LUCY'S
BIGGEST FISH TO FRY

LUCY'S
BIGGEST FISH TO FRY

A HUSBAND'S JOURNEY THROUGH
HIS WIFE'S FIGHT WITH BRAIN CANCER

*A Resource for Surviving Outcomes
that You Can't Affect*

Tom Stockburger

iUniverse LLC
Bloomington

LUCY'S BIGGEST FISH TO FRY
A Husband's Journey through His Wife's Fight with Brain Cancer

iUniverse books may be ordered through booksellers or by contacting:

iUniverse LLC
1663 Liberty Drive
Bloomington, IN 47403
www.iuniverse.com
1-800-Authors (1-800-288-4677)

ISBN: 978-1-4759-9773-6 (sc)
ISBN: 978-1-4759-9774-3 (ebk)

Library of Congress Control Number: 2013912651

Printed in the United States of America

iUniverse rev. date: 07/17/2013

CONTENTS

For Lucy's unconditional love
and her greatest accomplishments,
Keely and Kyle.

ACKNOWLEDGEMENTS

I would like to extend my deep gratitude to, and love for, my daughter, Keely, and son, Kyle. Thank you for always being there during this long, frustrating, and rewarding journey. Your unconditional love and understanding made it much easier for me to write this memoir of my experiences during the last chapter of your mother's too short life. Jake, thank you for standing by Keely and our family.

A special thanks to the friends and families in the Knolls neighborhood of southern Denver. 25 years ago we began friendships that will never end. Thank you for everything from the dinners, rides, house sitting, and gardening to the companionship, love, and support. Thanks to neighbor Christie at Duke who provided access to world renowned neuro-oncologist support.

To my cancer counselor, Jeanne, and all the professional caregivers on Lucy's team—including the folks at the University Of Colorado Cancer Center—a heartfelt thanks for providing the highest level of care possible. Thanks to my grief counselor, Annamarie and to Jeanne and Anne for their kind comments.

Deep appreciation goes to my dear Montana pals, Shellie, Barry, Kathleen, Phoebe, Tall Paul, the Plebe, Gael, and Doug, as well as my brother, Paul, and his wife, Carla. You all helped keep me sane as I balanced writing this book and managing my grief with dipping my toes into the dating world and trying to be a good father.

Thanks to my mom for being the non-sugarcoating and compassionate beacon who helped me stay on course as Lucy's caregiver. Your candor, love, and compassion means so much to Keely, Kyle, and me. I love you, Mom.

A special thanks to Lucy's sister, Shirley, who stood by me in a way that would have made Lucy very proud. Shirley's son

Kenny and his wife Deborah provided valuable guidance with the book—I'm still your Uncle Tom.

Sarah from Ex Libris Editing, LLC provided wonderful suggestions and editing support—thank you for cleaning up my grammar in a way that even my English major pal would appreciate.

INTRODUCTION

I n sickness and in health; these vows make a lot more sense now than they did in 1975 when Lucy and I were full of love and great expectations for a long and happy life together. Lucy passed away at home on August 14, 2011, just eight days before our 36th wedding anniversary after a 32 month battle with brain cancer.

During that period, Lucy had four brain surgeries, multiple chemotherapy and radiation treatments, and two gamma knife procedures. We consulted with some of the leading brain cancer specialists in the world and followed the gold standard of care, which resulted in Lucy outliving the initial prognosis by almost two years.

Throughout the cancer fight, I sent regular updates to Lucy's vast network of friends, family, and clients. I wrote each update based on the most recent events and then had her look them over before sending them. Frankly, Lucy was not up to writing regular updates and wanted me to do this for her. Additionally, writing the updates provided me great therapeutic value. They were a way to relieve my stress, and they kept me focused on providing Lucy with the best care I knew how to give.

It is my sincere hope that my story will help others facing a similar ordeal, although there is no right or wrong way to deal with the treatment, and in many cases, the loss—especially for the first time.

As I told my children, Keely and Kyle, "You have experienced one of the hardest things you'll ever have to deal with in your life, and there is no right or wrong way to grieve—fact is, many find their way *on* their way."

During our 37 years together, whenever I found myself worrying about my job, about painting our living room the right color, or about defending my political views with my conservative father, Lucy always brought me back to the important things in life—like love, our relationship, and our children—by saying, "Tom, you have bigger fish to fry." And, in a real sense, this book could have been titled *Tom's Biggest Fish to Fry.*

CHAPTER 1

A REAL, LIFE CHANGING EVENT

On Sunday morning, January 4, 2009, after we finished our coffee, Lucy decided to go to the grocery store to pick up who knows what. That was odd—I was usually the one that was sent with a list of things to buy. But, even odder was the fact that Lucy was back just fifteen minutes later, saying that when she walked into the store, she had been overpowered by smells and thought she was going to puke.

"Why don't you take a snooze?" I asked.

"That would be good. Then we can go to the mall and take back your pants and stop by the cell phone store to get Kyle a new phone," she replied.

A few hours later, the pants exchange was cut short when Lucy suddenly said, "I can't stand being here. It's so closed in." Before I could react, she continued, "Let's go." That sounded good to me, and I figured we could stop at the cell phone store another time, but she wasn't interested in going home yet. "No, Tom, we're out, and I really want to do this."

It was my first time to this cell phone store. We signed up for service and were put in a queue for the next available sales rep. Twenty minutes later, when our name was only two names from the top of the list, Lucy held up the most expensive phone in the store and said, "I'm going to buy this one."

I looked at her, and my eyes said, "You've got to be kidding me!" Just the day before we had talked about watching our spending, and Lucy already had a very nice cell phone.

Several minutes later, I turned around, and Lucy was looking at the queue display. Suddenly, her eyes rolled back, and I watched as she started to fall. I caught her, thinking she was having a stroke or some type of seizure and yelled, *"Someone call 911!"* As I laid her down she began to shake violently. The hustle and bustle of the showroom went silent, and I shouted once more, *"Call 911!"* Surprisingly, it wasn't the store workers who called for help, but a person standing next to us who used his cell phone.

I felt helpless not knowing what to do. "You're going to be all right, hang in there, help is on the way." I said. My mind was racing. First came the reality that Lucy was really in trouble. My next thought was that she might die. Irrationally, I thought I had somehow caused her collapse and seizure by giving her that "you've got to be kidding me" look.

The person who was on with 911 told me that paramedics were on their way.

A teenage girl came to me and asked, "Do I have your permission to help? I'm trained in CPR."

"Of course, thank you," I quickly replied.

Lucy's purse had fallen but she still had her glasses on. The teenage girl took Lucy's glasses off and put them into her purse. Next, she asked people to give us room.

As she shook, Lucy started to bite her tongue, and the blood quickly caused her to choke—after a short time, her face turned blue, and she stopped breathing.

"What should we do?" I asked the guy on the phone with the paramedics. Relayed through the man, the 911 operator told us to roll Lucy onto her side and hold her mouth open. The teenage girl and I got her on her side, and I held Lucy's chin down while the girl held her face. The blood drained out of her mouth, and she began to breath.

The paramedics arrived within minutes and quickly confirmed that Lucy had experienced a seizure. Two firemen carrying a gurney followed the paramedics inside. When they tried to lift Lucy onto it, she refused to cooperate.

"I'll be fine. Just let me lie here on the floor for a minute," she said. Finally, the paramedics convinced her she needed to sit up and that she would be more comfortable sitting up on the gurney. Reluctantly, she did as they suggested, and the paramedics promptly strapped her down and readied her for transport to the emergency room. Still, Lucy was not being very cooperative and said, "I just need to rest a minute, and then I can go home. I am not going to the hospital."

Seeing her resolve, one of the paramedics said, "She's out of immediate danger so we can take our time getting to the hospital." The paramedics let me know that they would transport Lucy in the ambulance without lights and sirens and that I could either ride with them or follow in my car.

Somewhat relieved that Lucy's condition did not warrant full lights, sirens and speeding to the hospital, I said, "Good, I'll follow you in my car."

I parked my car while the paramedics moved her from the ambulance to the ER admissions area. She was immediately moved into an exam room, and while we waited for the doctor, I called the kids. I told them that their mom had had a seizure, but was all right, and that tests were being conducted, and they should come down.

All of the tests, including the CAT scan, came back negative.

"*Hmmmm,*" said the ER doctor. "Do you drink?"

"Yes," Lucy replied.

"How much per day?" he asked. Lucy felt this was a tricky question to answer, because she believed that, no matter what number you answered with, the doctor would either double or triple it.

"Usually about one glass of wine a day," she answered. I was so flipped out about the seizure that I felt it was no time to hold back the truth that over the holidays it had been more than one glass a day.

"Well, did you have a big New Years?" the doctor asked.

Reluctantly, Lucy said, "Yes."

"Okay, I think you had an alcoholic seizure. I'll give you some anti-seizure medication until you can see your regular doctor," he replied.

Lucy was very upset with his diagnosis. Both Lucy and I knew it was not an alcoholic seizure, but I thought that it was not worth an argument with the doctor.

"Honey, let's not worry about this right now and just get you home," I said, hoping to calm her. By this time, Keely and Kyle were there, and both were really upset as they had never seen their mom in the ER or in this situation before. They had cut Lucy's fleece sweater off of her to get the IV started, and oddly, that was all that Lucy talked about while we waited for the discharge paperwork.

Lucy and I got in the car and drove to the pharmacy to get her anti-seizure meds. While the script was being filled we drove to get Lucy some French fries. As soon as Lucy finished her French fries and I picked up the meds, we made phone calls while driving home. Lucy called her sister, Shirley, while I called my mom. We wanted to let them know that Lucy had had a seizure and that we were waiting to learn more about what had caused it.

When we got home, Lucy said that her sister had suggested the possibility that a change in one of her daily meds from brand name to generic had caused her to have a reaction. In the hopes of finding something out, we ended up sending off both the brand name and generic drugs to Shirley, and she had her pharmacist do some type of test. We found out later in the week that the test showed no difference in the meds.

We even considered the idea that Lucy's seizure might have had something to do with the peanut brittle that my mom had sent us. I had felt a little woozy after eating some, and it was the only thing we had eaten in common Sunday morning. However, it eventually became apparent that my wooziness had been self-induced. I had always been susceptible to being influenced about how I felt—for example, if my dad ever asked, "Are you feeling okay, Tom?" I would usually think about it and then start to feel woozy. In other words, the peanut brittle was fine, and my discomfort was a result of overthinking as we tried to figure out what had caused Lucy's attack.

Lucy's biggest concern at this point was to avoid having another seizure. In the meantime, I spent a little time on the internet looking up what to do if she had another seizure—of course, if I hadn't been so distracted by the whole situation, I would have remembered that I could have just asked Lucy. After teaching for the Red Cross for many years, she would have known exactly what to do.

I had a tough time falling asleep that night—I kept thinking that my giving Lucy one of those *looks* had caused her seizure. Of course, when I told Lucy this later, she just laughed and said, "Nice try, Tom. You don't have that much power."

CHAPTER 2

First thing Monday morning, after making an appointment with Lucy's regular doctor, I called my mom, a retired nurse, to let her know that Lucy had slept well through the night. Following my father's death in 2006, my mom and I had begun talking two to three times a week, and I relied on her for support.

Lucy had six massage clients scheduled on Monday and called each to cancel. Later in the day, she asked me to call and cancel her appointments for the rest of the week. At Lucy's request, I told her clients that she had experienced a seizure and that, until she found out the cause, she would not be doing any massage.

That afternoon, I took Lucy to see her family care doctor. I asked if she wanted me to go with her into the exam, but she bravely said no. This would be the last time that I did not go into an exam with her.

After the doctor had read the ER report and examined Lucy, the doctor told her that she had not had an alcoholic seizure and that she needed to get an appointment with a neurologist right away.

When we got home, Lucy called her sister, and I called my mom again. My mom was very positive and optimistic and said we were doing the right things to find out the cause of what had happened.

The great thing about support from my mom during this journey was that she never sugarcoated anything, but at the same time, she kept me focused so I didn't get too wound up while we waited for more information from the doctors. She was my sounding board and provided an empathetic, but pragmatic ear as I dealt with each step. I have no doubt that this journey, as hard as it was, would have been even more difficult if it hadn't been for my mom's support.

Both Lucy and I felt better that her doctor had validated our belief that that she did not have an alcoholic seizure; however, both of us felt uneasy about being referred so quickly to a neurologist. Lucy reviewed the list of neurologists given by her doctor and decided to call the only woman on the list first thing in the morning.

CHAPTER 3

TAKING CHARGE OF LUCY'S CARE

On the second day after the seizure, Lucy took the list of neurologists referred by her doctor and called the woman neurologist she had selected the night before. After calling the neurologist she wanted, Lucy seemed very distracted and said she did not make an appointment because the earliest appointment was a month away. When I asked her if she had called the others, she said that she hadn't. This seemed odd since Lucy was always very proactive when it came to her health. I had a feeling that she was not quite herself and decided it would be helpful for me to take a very active role in helping get to the bottom of this seizure business.

With that in mind, I told Lucy that I would make the appointment. After talking with the other neurologists on the list, I called her first choice back and made an appointment for February 5th—it turned out that this was the earliest appointment of all the doctors. I decided that, from here on out, I needed to be very proactive, especially when I felt that Lucy was not quite 100%.

I also decided that I would go into each exam with Lucy because two sets of ears would be better than one, and I wanted to make sure I knew as much as I could about what was going on with her. I let Lucy know that this was my plan, and she agreed. I also made the resolution to take notes during the appointments, which ended up being helpful for many reasons, including giving the doctor a clear message that we were very serious about understanding what was going on.

The more I thought about us waiting for a month to learn what caused the seizure, the more I got nervous about what we would do to pass the time. I knew Lucy would be consumed by the waiting, so three days after the seizure, I called the neurologist's office again and talked with her nurse about getting in as soon as possible. My many years in sales had taught me that it was always better to take the initiative rather than wait, especially when I knew that it would be a long month waiting. When Lucy and I lived in Montana, we always said that January was the two longest months of the year because it was so cold and dark for 31 days; waiting for the appointment seemed very analogous.

A big part of my plan to be proactive was to make sure I learned the doctor's nurse's name and to establish a good relationship with her. During the call, I turned on the charm, but in a nice way, and I let the neurologist's nurse, Christy, know that we would take any cancellation and gave her my number. An hour later, she called back and told us that the neurologist could see us in an hour. I'm not saying that my turning on the charm helped, but moving the appointment from February 5th to January 7th was important.

Within an hour we were at the doctor's office. The neurologist conducted her normal exam and asked Lucy many questions. She then immediately ordered a MRI and an EEG to look at Lucy's brain waves. She also prescribed a new anti-seizure drug, noting that Lucy should never have been prescribed what the ER doctor had prescribed because she had not had an alcoholic seizure. Before we left, the neurologist directed her nurse to call the hospital in order make the appointment for the MRI.

After several days, I still had not heard from the neurologist's office about the test schedule, so I put my proactive hat back on and called the nurse and left a message. She called back and apologized for not getting back to us sooner and told me that she would get right on scheduling the test. The next day she called to let us know the hospital had scheduled Lucy for her tests and that the MRI and EEG would be taking place the next week, just ten days after Lucy's seizure.

Both Lucy and I knew instinctively that getting answers sooner than later on health issues was important. Time can be an ally in terms of early detection and treatment if the cause is something that can be treated.

CHAPTER 4

"HERE'S WHY YOU HAD THE SEIZURE"

Lucy had the MRI as scheduled. At her appointment the previous week, the neurologist had directed us to bring the MRI film to her office immediately after the procedure, so we waited at the hospital until it was ready. Once we had been given the film, we drove over to the neurologist's office. Lucy stayed in the car while I ran them in, but the neurologist wanted to look at the film right away, so I went and got Lucy. Looking back, I am sure that the neurologist had received a call from the radiologist at the hospital and already knew that there was a tumor.

Once we were settled in her office, the neurologist told us that the EEG results were normal. Then she put one of the films on her screen and moments later said, "Here's why you had the seizure; you have a tumor in this area."

Lucy jumped up to take a closer look, and I could see from where I was sitting that there was what looked like a small white smear on the left side of her brain. I immediately began to get choked up. Both the neurologist and Lucy gave me a look that said, "Hold on, Tom. No jumping to conclusions."

The neurologist told us that the tumor should be immediately removed and referred us to a neurosurgeon. The neurologist also said that she didn't feel the tumor was cancerous, but only the biopsy would tell for sure. Luckily, the tumor was close to the surface, and its location in the brain meant that side effects were unlikely. The neurologist then told us about some of the symptoms commonly associated with having a brain tumor, including nausea, headaches, vision changes, and changes in personality. She asked Lucy if she had noticed any of these.

Lucy immediately mentioned our recent Thanksgiving dinner with Keely's boyfriend's family. Shortly after getting to Jake's parent's house, Lucy had said that she didn't feel well and was nauseous. She went outside to get some air and then returned and sat down to eat. But, as the food was being passed around, Lucy had once again excused herself and gone back outside to get some air. I had checked on her, and she had told me that she felt like she was going to get sick. Thinking that Lucy had some bug, we had given our apologies and cut our stay short.

Lucy also recalled several weeks in December when she hadn't been feeling well and had cancelled some of her client appointments, thinking she had come down with a cold. Some of Lucy's clients later told us that they were surprised by this since many had had several appointments cancelled, and this was not like Lucy, who rarely got sick.

Driving home from the neurologist appointment, we talked about how Lucy's annual four wheel trip to the mountains with her best buddy Char had not gone well the previous summer—after returning home, they hadn't talked until Lucy's birthday in October. There had been a definite change in the way Lucy acted with Char that trip, but at the time, no one had known what was happening.

Again, looking back, I should have given more attention to Lucy's nausea and minor personality changes.

As we drove home, we were both still stunned. It was a very quiet drive, and what little discussion there was centered on what and how to tell the kids. Lucy was clear about the fact that she believed we had to be honest with them and not necessarily sugarcoat anything.

Kyle was scheduled to go to New York City to audition in front of some 30+ MFA graduate schools the following week. Kyle's passion was to become either an actor or writer on Broadway. He received a Bachelor's of Fine Arts degree with an emphasis in acting and was looking to expand his talent and experience for acting, singing, dancing and writing with a Masters of Fine Arts.

The audition was designed to showcase his acting talent with the hope that he would land a scholarship for graduate school. Lucy was adamant that the surgery, no matter when it was scheduled, should not interrupt Kyle's plans since he had been preparing for the auditions for the previous five months, not to mention the four years he spent at CU earning his BFA. I agreed with Lucy about Kyle and being honest with them.

Both Keely and Kyle were home when we returned home from the doctor's office, and we sat down and let them know what was going on. They were both as stunned by the news as we had been and still were, and there was lots of hugging and crying. Keely decided to quit her new job so that she could stay home to help care for Lucy, but, as agreed, we told Kyle that he needed to go to NYC for his auditions, regardless of the surgery schedule. He was obviously reluctant to keep his audition, but we were insistent, and he finally agreed.

After talking with the kids about the surgery, and once Lucy was settled in for a nap, I called the neurosurgeon's office and made an appointment for the following Monday, January 19th.

I then asked to speak with the neurosurgeon's surgery scheduler. I explained the situation and asked about the earliest possible surgery date. The nurse told me that his surgery days were Monday and Wednesday and that January had typically been a slow month for surgeries. Since we were coming in Monday January 19th I asked about surgery on Wednesday January 21st—she said it was wide open, and I did my charming thank you. I then asked if it would be helpful for me to bring in the MRI films ahead of the appointment, and she said yes.

Leaving Lucy, who was still napping, at home, I took the film to the neurosurgeon's office. While I was there, I asked to see his nurse and let her know that we really appreciated her help, and I picked up the new patient forms to save time the day of the appointment.

It had been a difficult day. Lucy was relieved to know what caused the seizure, but we were both scared by the possibility that it might be cancer, although neither of us said that—we didn't want the kids to go over the edge.

CHAPTER 5

LET'S HAVE A BRAIN SURGERY SHOWER

Even though only a few days had passed, our friends in the neighborhood, led by our friend Sally G, had already started coordinating a meals on wheels cooking schedule. Until Lucy was back on her feet, they wanted to make sure that we didn't have to deal with the burden of cooking.

Additionally, since our friends knew we would most likely be having the surgery next week, Lucy's closest neighborhood girlfriends scheduled a pre-surgery shower for Sunday January 18th. Lucy and her group of girlfriends always rallied behind whoever needed help and support, whether that help was for someone whose husband was going to be on business travel for several weeks or to aid in organizing a pantry dinner when we were all stuck and couldn't get to the store during a major snowstorm. When that happened, we'd grab whatever was in our pantry or freezer and walk to someone's house for dinner, kids and all.

Several years before, Lucy and the girlfriends had arranged a weekend getaway for one of the girls who had to have brain surgery (her tumor turned out to be benign). When the girls went to the airport to meet their friend who was to have the operation, the welcoming girlfriends had toilet paper wrapped around their heads trying to look like they just had brain surgery.

Lucy received some very nice cards, a couple of cool hats, a few scarves, and some comfortable booties for the hospital stay.

Surgery Shower, from L to R—
Becky, Lucy, Debbie, Linda, Sally T, Jeanne, not pictured Sally G

While Lucy was at the surgery shower, the husbands took me to a nearby sports bar to watch some Sunday afternoon football.

The guys were very supportive, but really at a loss when it came to what to say. I enjoyed being able to take a breather from the whirlwind of non-stop activity centered on Lucy's seizure and tumor, but I just couldn't let myself go and relax and watch football because I knew that the next week was going to be very stressful.

As the boys and I watched football, chatted, and had a few beers, I kept looking at the people in the bar. I thought, little do they know what is going on in my life with my wife's brain tumor. It gave me pause to wonder what stresses they each had and how they were able to put them away for a while, if at all.

Later that evening, Lucy and I talked candidly about the seizure and upcoming surgery. She had always been very health conscious and, from her arthroscopic knee surgery to her hysterectomy, had learned as much as she could about the health issues she experienced. This was the first time that I felt a deep sense of fear from Lucy, though. She was truly afraid that it was cancer.

Irrationally, I still felt like I had caused the seizure, if not by my giving her that *look* at the cell phone store, then by having been tough to live with over the years.

I kept reliving the scene at the cell phone store—the seizure, Lucy turning blue as she stopped breathing, and, finally, her return to consciousness.

During one of our chats in the days before the surgery, I told Lucy that I felt each moment with her after the seizure was a gift. I often expressed this thought to her and others—it became my day-to-day mantra. I looked at each new moment with Lucy as a blessing. I even started praying and regularly recited the Lord's Prayer throughout the journey and beyond.

CHAPTER 6

My job involved selling software solutions to state and local government, and it usually took 18-24 months to build relationships before I really hit my stride in terms of making sales and meeting my annual sales target. At the time of Lucy's seizure, I had been with my current company for two years. The year 2009 was my make or break year, which meant that either I hit my sales target, or I would be looking for a new job.

Fortunately, I was working for one of the best companies to work for in America according to one of the leading business magazines. This privately owned company had a reputation for providing world-class employee benefits, including low cost, benefit-rich health insurance. In addition to the benefits provided by my company, I learned about how the federal Family Medical Leave Act (FMLA) provided up to 12 weeks of protected time off and ensured my job when I returned.

During my 32 years working in the information technology industry, I had never been in a position where I might have to take an extended period of time off. Money had been tight for us in the years leading up to the diagnosis, and I was concerned that if I had to take time off, it would add additional stress, even with the generous company health benefits including paid sick time off.

Right after the seizure, I called my boss and let him know what was going on and that there was a chance I would miss the annual, national sales kickoff meeting the week of January 19th. He was very supportive and told me to take whatever time I needed. I had known him for over 25 years, and he had recruited me to this current company. He let his boss, the vice president of sales, know what was going on as well. The vice president of sales called me and gave her support to my decision to miss the annual kickoff meeting.

The vice president also told me that she was transferring me to a different sales region and that I would get a new boss. This news added some stress. Since I knew 2009 was a make or break year, the idea of having a new boss who did not know me was unnerving. One item in my favor was that I had an excellent business relationship with the vice president and could go to her with any concerns.

Knowing that in 2009 I had to meet or exceed my sales target or lose my job, I decided to use my sales experience and communication skills to keep my bosses well informed about Lucy's health. In effect, I was selling my management on keeping me employed.

Our 401K plan had taken a big hit with the recession and if I had to change jobs, there was still plenty of power within the health insurance industry to not have to cover pre-existing conditions.

The Friday before Lucy's surgery, I called my new boss and let him know that I was not going to be able to go to North Carolina for the kickoff. After thinking it over, I had decided that a new manager and potentially losing my job were the least of my worries; as Lucy said at the time, "You have bigger fish to fry."

CHAPTER 7

"YES, IT REALLY IS BRAIN SURGERY"

Over the weekend, Lucy, the kids, and I had maintained our optimism. The surgery shower and my guy's day out had helped pass the time. Still, what we were facing could not be put away on a shelf, and it was difficult to have a truly relaxing moment.

On Monday morning, we met with the neurosurgeon. He discussed the nature of the surgery and repeated the neurologist's assurance that the surgery would be low-risk since the tumor was close to the surface and in a relatively safe part of the brain. The only potential side effect was the possibility of some loss in Lucy's peripheral vision in her left eye. He then suggested that she have the surgery sooner than later and said that he would check with his nurse to see how his schedule looked over the next week or so.

"How about Wednesday?" I asked. "I understand that your schedule looks good that day."

"Who have you been talking to?" he asked, giving me a funny look.

I told him I had already chatted with his nurse, and he started to laugh. I said that from what I understood, early action was a good thing when it came to brain surgery. He agreed and left the room for a few minutes and came back still smiling.

"Nice work, Tom. Wednesday works."

He then described the process, the procedure, and how long he estimated that Lucy would be in the hospital. He said that the entire surgery process would take at least four hours. The day of the surgery would begin with Lucy having another MRI. We would then have to wait while they reviewed the MRI results and completed their computer mapping process. Once that was complete, Lucy would be moved to the surgery room where they would position her for the surgery. The actual surgery would take about an hour and a half, and it would take another two hours to close.

The neurosurgeon suggested we contact an oncologist and recommended one associated with the hospital where the surgery would be performed. Although we didn't know yet whether or not the tumor was cancerous, he reasoned that it would be good to already have a relationship with an oncologist should the worst come to pass. The neurosurgeon also told us that Lucy would be in the hospital for two to four days and that the first two would be spent in the ICU.

When we got back home from the neurosurgeon's office, I called the oncologist and made an appointment for the week following the surgery. I also asked if I could stop by and pick up the new patient forms prior to the surgery. The receptionist told me that this would be no problem and commended me for being proactive.

On Tuesday morning, we got a call from the hospital informing us that we were to check in on Wednesday at 10:15 AM and that the surgery would start around 1:30 PM.

Lucy was very happy that the surgery would be in just two days and called her sister and other friends to let them know. Her sister immediately made a reservation to fly in from Seattle. While Lucy was on the phone, I called my mom to let her know the most recent news. She reminded me that the tumor's location in a safe place meant that Lucy would most likely come through the surgery with no trouble at all. My mom knew that I had a tendency to worry excessively and overreact to health related matters and sensed in my voice that this was the case, so she told me not to get too wigged out until we knew more about the tumor.

Seventeen days after the seizure, Lucy would have the tumor removed. Over the next day and a half, we got ready for the surgery. This included canceling the remaining massage appointments with her clients and starting an email update list so that we could let friends and families know what was going on with Lucy's surgery and progress. However, even with the email list, we still called close friends and family to personally fill them in on the details.

On Tuesday, we took Kyle to the airport for his NYC trip and picked up Shirley when she arrived from Seattle. Dinner with Keely, her boyfriend, Jake, and Shirley was upbeat, and we all remained very positive.

For much of the rest of the night we watched the Presidential Inauguration events—Lucy had worked for Hillary Clinton in the primaries, and I supported Barak Obama. In any other situation, Lucy and I would have been celebrating the dawn of a new age for America, but our thoughts were elsewhere.

CHAPTER 8

The day of the surgery Lucy and I were up early. Just before 8:00 AM, we got a call from the hospital letting us know that the neurosurgeon's first surgery had been cancelled, and we were asked if it would be possible for us to get there right away. Within 20 minutes, Lucy and I were off to the hospital with Shirley and Keely planning on coming a little later.

When we got checked in at the hospital, they took Lucy in for her pre-op MRI. Once that was done, the surgical team reviewed the MRI, mapped out the surgery, and made their final preparations. While the surgical team made their preparations, Keely waited with Lucy in pre-op, and I brought in her sister and her dear friend Char. Lucy and Char had become fast friends over the past few years and had taken Char's Jeep on several four-wheeling trips over old mining roads high atop Colorado mountain passes.

Lucy was upbeat, but scared. I could tell that this was the case by her constant chatter, which included comments that had the pre-op folks laughing. For example, the surgeon's assistant was attractive, and Lucy told her to be wary of me hitting on her while Lucy was in the ICU. When Lucy took a bathroom break just before going in for surgery, she pulled her gown and mooned her friend Char to get just one more laugh.

After they wheeled Lucy in, the surgery nurse let us know that she would call my cell phone periodically during the surgery to update me on the progress. The people in the waiting room included Keely, Jake, Char, Char's husband Mike, Shirley, and Lucy's 2nd cousin Cindi. We settled in and waited.

About an hour later, the nurse called to let me know that they were almost finished doing the mapping, and she would let me know when the surgery started. She said that Lucy was doing well and hanging in there.

At this point, I was still scared, but I knew that Lucy was in such good physical condition that she should be fine through the surgery. I tried very hard not to show my fear and again reminded myself that each moment since the seizure had been a blessing.

Over the past two and a half weeks, I had experienced all kinds of emotions and thoughts regarding the various possible outcomes. The scenarios ranged from the tumor being benign to the possibility that it would be cancerous. Looking back, I think that playing out the possibilities in my mind was just one of the many ways that I tried to cope. It had all happened so fast that there was little time to decompress and digest the reality and seriousness of the seizure, brain tumor, and surgery.

The second call from the nurse let me know that they had started the surgery and that it would be about an hour to an hour and a half with another hour or so to close. I let everyone waiting know and we sent Jake out for burgers. I called my mom and kept her posted.

The third call let me know that they had removed the tumor and believed that they had achieved a good resection, which meant they thought they had taken the entire tumor out as well as a perimeter around it. The nurse also told me that Lucy had handled surgery just fine and that the neurosurgeon would be out after he closed and would give us more details. I hung up, and we settled in and waited some more. Later, the neurosurgeon came out and repeated what the nurse had told me about the resection being very clean and thorough. He also said that the tumor was a primary tumor, which meant it had originated in the brain. He explained that this could be a good thing since it meant that the cancer hadn't spread to the brain from another part of the body.

I asked what the tumor looked like, and he said it was definitely an astrocytoma, but he didn't know the grade or type. In the meantime, Lucy would be in recovery for an hour and then moved to the ICU. Once she was settled in the ICU, we would be able to see her.

My head was spinning. What was an astrocytoma, and what did the neurosurgeon mean by grades? I decided to get on the internet later when I got home.

I went in alone first to see Lucy in the ICU. She was fairly coherent with her head in a full bandage, but I was not quite prepared for how she looked with all the tubes and such. Lucy and I talked as best we could. She asked how the surgery had gone, and I told her that it had all gone well and that they believed they had removed all of the tumor, plus a perimeter around it. I also told her that the biopsy might take up to a week.

I brought Keely in before too long, but I made sure that before I brought her in, I prepped her on how her mom looked so that she wouldn't be too upset. After Keely had spent some time with Lucy, I shuffled Shirley and the others in for brief visits—I had taken on the role of traffic cop. By this point it was after 4:00 PM, and I asked Keely and Jake to go home and check on our dog, Sadie, and cat, Lily.

I stayed with Lucy as she drifted in and out of sleep. At 6:00 PM, the hospital kicked me out for a couple of hours which was standard policy during their nightly nursing staff shift change. I didn't want to leave, but I understood why they needed me to, so I went home and had some dinner with Keely, Jake, and Shirley, but I returned to Lucy's side as soon as I could.

CHAPTER 9

WHAT IS AN ASTROCYTOMA?

I left the ICU later that night around 11:00 PM, and when I got home, I anxiously got on my computer to find out more about astrocytomas. I quickly learned that there were four grades or types of astrocytomas. A grade 1 astrocytoma could be benign and wasn't much to worry about, especially when found in younger people. Grades 2 through 4, though, were cancerous. A grade 2 astrocytoma carried a median survival rate of five years, a grade 3 astrocytoma carried a median survival rate of 18 months, and a grade 4 astrocytoma carried a median survival rate of less than a year, although people had survived for three years.

After I had done my research on the internet, I found that Shirley was still awake. She let me know that she had also done some research on the internet. We sat down in the living room and compared notes.

First, we agreed that this was very serious. Next, we both believed that the astrocytoma was most likely a grade 4 based on the material we read about astrocytomas removed from women aged 55 to 60 in which a high percentage of the tumors were grade 4. Lucy was 56 years old at the time of her diagnosis. Additionally, the material we both read indicated that survival rates for grades 2-3 were best if detected in ages under 30. We both were hoping for the best, but the material on the internet was not very encouraging.

We talked about Senator Ted Kennedy's brain tumor, which had been detected after he had a similar seizure just seven months before. Senator Kennedy had been diagnosed with a type of grade 4 astrocytoma called a malignant glioma brain tumor.

After we talked for a while, I said goodnight to Shirley and composed my first update to Lucy's friends and family list before calling it a night.

January 21, 2009
Lucy's Surgery

> *Hi all—what a long day for Lucy and the rest of us. Lucy's surgery was successful in that they got a clean resection of the tumor and the surrounding perimeter. The neurosurgeon said the tumor was an astrocytoma and the type would be determined by the biopsy. Lucy is doing well and cracking jokes with the ICU nurses. As we learn more, I'll be sure to update you. Much love, Tom*

CHAPTER 10

THIS IS NOT GOOD NEWS

The next morning, Shirley and I got to ICU just after the oncologist and his internist had left after seeing Lucy. We chatted with Lucy for a few minutes before I called and left a message for the oncologist asking him call me.

I went back into the room and talked with Shirley and Lucy for about five more minutes before the oncologist returned my call. I excused myself to talk with him. He was very compassionate and let me know that the hospital radiologist thought that the astrocytoma was at least a grade 2, but that it may have some grade 4 in it as well. This was difficult to hear, but he let me know as kindly as possible and told me not to jump to any conclusions until CU Health Sciences weighed in. He also suggested that I contact his recommended radiologist to set an appointment since radiation would most likely be the next step.

I wondered what I should tell Lucy. It was very important to me to be honest with Lucy, but I also didn't want to worry her needlessly. Finally, I decided that, since the oncologist hadn't had any definite information and had told me not to jump to conclusions, it would be best to simply say that they didn't know yet. With as much as Lucy had been through over the past 18 days, she didn't need to know right then that this might be very serious.

When I returned to the room, Lucy and Shirley were anxiously waiting to hear what the oncologist had said. I told them that the results were inconclusive and that we may not know definitively for a week.

After Shirley and I left the ICU, I filled Shirley in on the rest of what the oncologist had told me. She was very upset by the time I had finished and was insistent that I tell Lucy right away. She was worried that my omission could really affect the trust between Lucy and me. I told Shirley not to worry and that, based on being with Lucy for the past 35 years and knowing her as well as I did, everything would be okay between Lucy and I when I eventually told her the additional details. I also told Shirley that I was not going to tell anyone else, not even our kids, until we had more information. I felt it was important not to burden the kids with the additional information until Lucy knew everything. I didn't want them to be in the position of having to lie or hold back from their mother. I also felt that Kyle didn't need any more stress while he was in the middle of his grad school auditions.

Lucy's progress recovering in the ICU was remarkable, something which the ICU nurses made sure to mention to us during our visits. Lucy's strong will, great attitude, excellent physical condition, and sense of humor were paying great dividends as she began her recovery from the surgery.

True to form, 24 hours after the surgery, Lucy sweetly demanded to be moved out of the ICU. I chatted with the surgeon's PA about this, and she said that it would be okay if I wanted to press the issue, but it was very rare for a craniotomy patient to only spend one day in the ICU. The ICU nurses were also reluctant to be supportive of moving Lucy out of the ICU after just one day, so I made another command decision and told Lucy that she would be staying in the ICU for a second night. Again, after thinking about it and talking with Shirley, Keely, and my mom, we all agreed that there should be no rush to get Lucy out of the ICU.

January 23, 2009 Update
Lucy Coming Home

On Friday, Lucy was moved to the surgery recovery floor and continued to recover very nicely. Based on her improvement, the surgeon said that she would be able to go home the next day.

Keely came to the hospital each day and brought little expressions of love and support including some flowers and a homemade card. Kyle continued his auditions for grad school in New York City and called daily to give his mom support.

During all of years parenting Keely and Kyle, we always used how they sounded as the barometer for how they were feeling, good or bad. With Keely at home, it was easy for us to hear in her voice that she was holding up well given the circumstances. We could tell by Kyle's voice over the phone from New York that he was doing no better than Keely.

Both kids had many forces at work affecting their stress levels—Keely being on the front lines with Lucy at home and Kyle being away from his mom and in the most important auditions of his budding career.

The evening before she came home, I sent an email out to Lucy's friends and family list.

> *All—once again, I cannot begin to express thanks for the feelings of love and support that each of you has expressed—these are the most difficult times that Lucy and our family has ever faced—even after 33+ years of trying to live with that Montana boy she met in Missoula . . . Lucy remains strong and ready to face what is next—the net at this point is that we are waiting for the experts at the University of Colorado Med School to weigh in on what type of tumor was removed on Wednesday . . . whatever the prognosis, we are ready to fight and take each day as a blessing, again the cup IS half full!*
>
> *I talked with the oncologist today and we have an appointment next Friday, the 30th, to learn what the experts say—in all likelihood, we may know sooner if the results come in before Friday and we will be sure to let you know.*
>
> *The dinners are great, although they are doing nothing for us to lose those holiday pounds!*
>
> *Lucy should be home tomorrow and she is looking forward to sleeping in her own bed . . . of course that means I get to sleep on the couch when she wakes me at 2:00am to let me know that the snoring keeps her awake . . . I'll take that over the past 3 nights with her at the hospital any day.*
>
> *As mentioned last night, for those of the Colorado folks, we appreciate you giving us a few days to let Lucy rest—pls*

call me if you plan on stopping by to say hello—you may just be able to say hello to me, Shirley, Keely or her boyfriend Jake.

In times like this we really learn to appreciate many things—Keely is so strong, caring and so much like Lucy yet so much her own person that Lucy and I thank God each day for her being here with us—she is supported by a young man we all adore who makes each day more special—thanks to the Jakester for being Jake, although Jake's parents are MSU grads, he is still okay. Good news on Kyle—he had a great audition for grad school at NYU today and made it past several call backs and it's looking very good for him at NYU (not just your regular grad school!)—when he called Lucy to tell her late today, this really brightened her day as much as the note Keely left at ICU when Lucy was sleeping. Kyle will continue his auditions in New York City through next Tuesday and he is really being a trooper by being able to balance his love for Lucy and us with being focused on his future which we insisted he continue to do. Lucy and I are committed to Keely and Kyle regardless of the hurdles we are facing.

Enough about us . . . what each of you has done makes each day easier for us to live—again many thanks and I'll look forward to sharing news as we learn it—Lucy sends her love to each of you and we'll chat soon—best, Tom

CHAPTER 11

THERAPEUTIC VALUE OF COMMUNICATING

I found that writing the updates for family and friends was very therapeutic for me as I tried to wrap my head around what had happened and what was happening. Less than three weeks had passed since Lucy's seizure, and already she was coming home from major surgery.

Writing the updates caused me to reflect deeply on what was going on with Lucy's health as well as how Lucy, Keely, Kyle, and I were doing emotionally with this. Giving information and updates on Lucy's health was the easy part, but articulating our emotions was tough. Still, it was useful in that it helped me keep focused on our emotional well-being.

The meals on wheels organized by the neighborhood were in full swing with Sally still handling the scheduling. This was such a great thing for our neighbors, friends, and family to do for us, in large part because it meant there was one less thing for me to worry about. I had started a list of who brought or sent food, flowers, or other expressions of support so that we could write thank you cards. Looking back, I see how important it was to keep current with the list, because with all the activity and stress it was easy to lose track of who had brought what and what dish needed to be returned to whom.

Once Lucy was home, we were focused on her recovery from surgery and getting ready to learn more about the tumor. Each day, Lucy grew stronger, and everyone was amazed at how well she was recovering.

With her recovering well, I decided that it was time to tell her what the oncologist had said about the tumor being at least a grade 2 astrocytoma with possibly some grade 4, but that we needed to wait for the official biopsy results to know for sure. I was relieved to have told her, but it turned out that she had already known something was up. Once I was done explaining that nothing was certain until the biopsy results came back, she peered into my eyes and said that when I had walked back into the ICU room after my call with the oncologist, I "looked like Timmy had just learned that Lassie had died."

CHAPTER 12

GRADE 4 CANCER

Friday, January 30th, a little short of three weeks after Lucy's seizure, we met with the oncologist to learn the results of the tumor biopsy. He was candid and professional while being compassionate, and he let us know right away that the expert at CU Health Sciences had determined that the astrocytoma tumor was a grade 4 cancer called Glioblastoma Multiform (GBM). This was the worst type of astrocytoma. I was stunned, and Lucy was silent—somehow, I think she had already known.

The oncologist went on to tell us that the prognosis was a survival rate of 12 months, but that with a new chemotherapy drug, the survival rate may be extended by one to three months. I started to cry. Lucy and the doctor seemed more concerned about my reaction than by how Lucy reacted.

Lucy's tumor was rare because it was much like a sunny side-up egg with grade 2 cancer being the egg white and the grade 4 GBM forming the yolk in the middle. The oncologist informed us that encapsulated tumors could have some impact on the survival rate and that he was bringing Lucy's case to the Hospital Tumor Board on February 12th to get additional input. He also planned to get regular consultation with the brain cancer research experts at CU Health Sciences.

After I regained my composure, I asked, "Does this type of cancer that has the grade 4 part encapsulated change the 12 month prognosis?" His response was candid, yet somewhat ambiguous. He told us that some people did better than the statistics and others did not, and he was quick to point out that while the statistics were not in our favor, miracles did happen.

As the conversation continued, we learned that the standard of care for this type of cancer was seven to eight weeks of radiation combined with chemotherapy. In most cases, the chemotherapy continued for months after the radiation was done. The oncologist also described clinical trials and told us that one or more of these might be an option going forward if the standard of care didn't prove to be as effective as we wanted. But, our next step was to meet with the oncology radiologist to get the radiation scheduled.

Our oncologist was affiliated with the hospital where the surgery had been done and told us that the hospital offered free cancer counseling for the families of patients. I got the contact information and made a note to call the counselor sooner rather than later.

It was the longest ten minute drive home in my life. For me, the impact of just learning that my wife of 34 years had terminal brain cancer was devastating—I could only imagine what Lucy was thinking. On the drive, we discussed how we should tell the kids. Lucy thought it would be best for her to tell them because it was her cancer and she wanted to tell them in a way that showed she was strong and confident about fighting the cancer. We then talked about how each kid would react—we knew that Keely would be more expressive and emotional, while Kyle would internalize his feelings. Above all, Lucy wanted us to be honest with them. She didn't want to sugarcoat the prognosis, but she also didn't want to give either of them the impression that we were giving up in any way, shape, or form. Fortunately, Kyle was home from New York, so at least both of our kids would hear the same thing from us at the same time.

Lucy had always been the parent who handled the tough conversations and this would be her toughest.

When we arrived at home, we sat the kids down, and Lucy told them the prognosis without mincing words. She went on to tell them about the treatment plan and that she was going to fight this with all of her resources.

After some group hugs and crying, we all fell silent, and Keely and Kyle immediately began processing the most life-changing news that they had ever heard.

Later, Lucy told us that she was going to get a medical marijuana license and take advantage of at least one perk of having cancer. This brought some short lived smiles from us all.

January 30, 2009 Update
Big "C" Word

Below is the email that I sent out to our friends and family network following Lucy's official diagnosis:

> *Today we met with the oncologist and he let us know that the tumor is a stage 4 brain cancer called a Glioblastoma Multiform (GBM). The good news is that the stage 4 portion of the tumor is encapsulated by stage 2 which means that the stage 4 cancer is surrounded much like a sunny side up egg with the white being stage 2 and the yolk being stage 4. This is a rare type and offers some hope. The prognosis is not good with most GBM patients having a 12 month survival rate. Lucy will be starting radiation and chemotherapy sessions as soon as she fully heals from the surgery. Our spirits are as good as can be expected and we are preparing for the fight. We appreciate your continued prayers and all expressions of support, and will keep you updated when she starts the treatments.*
>
> *With much love, Tom*

CHAPTER 13

SLEEPING BETTER, ORGANICALLY

With a month to recuperate before starting the chemo and radiation, Lucy and I tried to get our heads wrapped around what lay ahead.

When a person is first diagnosed with cancer, the oncologist is usually quick to prescribe sleep aids so that the person is not up all night ruminating about what lies ahead—there is a very obvious inclination to overthink everything, especially one's own mortality. However, neither Lucy nor I had ever been fans of any type of prescription sleep aid and declined any scripts for sleep aids.

Being an old pot head from the '70s, Lucy followed through with her previous declaration and asked the oncologist to write her a script for medical marijuana. As she had told our children, she had decided that cancer had at least one perk, and she was going to take full advantage of the fact that medical marijuana was legal in Colorado. It had a few advantages, including the fact that it helped Lucy sleep without prescription sleep aids. With a couple of puffs of marijuana and a glass or two of wine, sleep came easily with no side effects in the morning.

Even as I supported anything that helped Lucy feel better, I made sure to discuss the use of alcohol and marijuana with the oncologist, the radiologist, and the neurologist. I wanted to be sure that nothing interfered with her treatment, but the doctors let me know that, with her prognosis, wine and pot were the least of our worries. However, they also advised me that alcohol didn't typically mix well with the chemotherapy drug and that most people who tried to combine the two ended up getting very sick. As such, when the chemo began, the wine was left in the rack.

As the primary caregiver, I decided early on that I needed to be as clear-minded as I could to make sure that Lucy got the best support and care possible. While I am no saint when it comes to the use of alcohol and pot, I was initially very careful about the use of either, knowing that at any time I might need to rush her to the hospital or have a serious call with one of the doctors. Furthermore, my mission to make sure that Lucy had the best care available gave me the strength not to immediately go down the self-medicating path, something that would have been easy to do. I also needed to set a good example for my kids. They were reeling enough from the reality of the initial prognosis and didn't need their dad flipping out.

Lucy and I discussed Lucy's use of the marijuana with our kids and related the doctors' words about this being the least of our worries. We had always had a very open and honest relationship with our kids, and how we treated this matter was no exception.

While I am not necessarily advocating the use of medical marijuana during the treatment of this type of brain cancer, I am convinced that it helped Lucy. Once she started using it, she had no trouble sleeping, and with her sleeping some 12 hours a night, her body was able to rest and recuperate. Rest, in my opinion, was an ally.

CHAPTER 14

While Lucy was recovering from her surgery, I began to put our financial house in order so that there would be minimal financial stress on us as we dealt with this new chapter in our life.

As soon as we found out about the cancer, one of the first things I did was help Lucy apply for disability as offered by the Social Security Administration. Lucy had paid into this fund for many years and, once her application was approved, she received a monthly disability check that really helped us meet our expenses.

After getting the contact information from the oncologist, I also started seeing the cancer counselor. One of the things we discussed was financial stress, and she provided some resources that were available for small cash donations, as well as organizations that offered vacation homes for free.

As noted previously, my employer had been very generous about giving me as much time and flexibility possible during the first year so that I could support Lucy. I had also received a guarantee from my vice president about not worrying about hitting my 2009 sales target. As such, I was able to keep working with my generous base salary and fantastic benefits.

During Lucy's almost 3 year battle with the cancer, we only paid co-pays and never had any push-back from the insurance company on any treatments. The owners of the privately held company I worked for always said they wanted their 14,000+ employees to have the best benefits available, and they walked the walk! Having this security for the first year helped reduce my level of stress beyond description.

However, even with my generous salary and Lucy's massage therapy income, things had been very tight financially for several years. We were like many Americans at the time, living from paycheck to paycheck. Plus, our 401K had taken a major hit with the recession.

Knowing that things were about to grow even tighter with Lucy's lost income, I went to my bank of 40 years and asked if we could either reduce the interest rates on our loans or extend the terms. My bank had received over $6.5B in bailout funds from our government, and I was hoping that they would be as generous to me in my time of trouble as the American people had been to them. I must have been dreaming. I even offered to use Lucy's life insurance policy as collateral, but to no avail. Suffice it to say, the first chance I got, I changed banks.

I also called my credit union. I had a car loan with them, and after I explained my situation, they asked what I could afford to pay per month on the loan. I said $200 a month and they kindly said that would be fine. Their understanding helped me reduce my payments by over $300 per month.

To help our cash flow, I took out a loan from my 401K. Typically, when the Big C comes into your life, friends and family are quick to offer "whatever you need." These very nice gestures can turn into real eye openers when you actually ask for help. For example, I went to one person who had offered, knowing he could afford to help. I asked to borrow money using Lucy's life insurance policy as the collateral. Well, as it turned out, I was told, "I don't lend money to close friends or family." This created a very uncomfortable situation for both of us, but I was not the one who had said "anything" to help. Thankfully, one of my family members made a genuine offer to help, and we received a generous cash gift.

I never thought I'd be asking people for financial help. While it was very uncomfortable, I decided that I had to do whatever was necessary to make Lucy's life as stress-free as possible and financial stress had been one of biggies over the past several years. I even evaluated selling Lucy's life insurance policy, but could only get 30 cents on the dollar.

The most positive "eye opener" occurred when I reached out to one of my Sigma Chi fraternity brothers for help. We had always been a loyal group, and membership in the group extended beyond college. For example, if anyone ever asked me if I "was" in a fraternity in college, I would answer with the standard Sigma Chi answer, "It's not that I *was* a member; I *am* a Sigma Chi." Still, it wasn't until Lucy's ordeal that these bonds were truly tested.

Back in college, I took one of my Sigma Chi brothers out for a beer or two on his 21st birthday. Halfway through the first beer, he turned to me and said, "Hey, Stocks (my fraternity nickname), what's a guy to do with $21.6 million dollars that he gets when he turns 21?" My answer was quick and to the point: "You buy the next round." Even though I had not seen or talked with this fraternity brother in three years, I called him late one afternoon and explained the situation, including using the life insurance as collateral. He said he was in a meeting and that he'd call me back in the morning. When he called back the next morning, he asked for my address. Two days later, I got a check and a note to saying no need to worry about any collateral.

When I paid the loan back after Lucy died, I sent him a check with interest. He sent me back a check for most of the interest and a nice note saying, "Brothers don't charge brothers interest." I used the money from his check in two ways—first, to become a life loyal (life-time) member of the Sigma Chi fraternity, and second, to enroll Lucy and I as life-time members of the University of Montana Alumni Association.

February 23, 2009 Update
Treatment Begins

As we got into full treatment mode, I used email updates to let friends and family know what was going on especially if there was significant news—in many cases however; the updates provided me some "Tom time" to decompress and regroup my thoughts about how Lucy, Keely, Kyle, and I were dealing with the cancer.

> *Good evening everyone—it's been awhile since the last update and we wanted to let you know how it's going. First of all, we cannot thank each and every one of you enough for your love, prayers, support, cookies, soup, wonderful dinners,*

cards, books, dvd's, flowers, thoughts, positive energy, sunshine and cheesecake . . . I could go on as you know.

Last Wednesday Lucy started the chemotherapy which will last 4-6 months. She takes a pill each night before bed and seems to be tolerating it well with the help from anti-nausea med. We were told that 55% of the patients using this chemo will lose their hair—well, this will be no of surprise to you, Lucy decided that if she starts to lose her hair then why not just take care of this now; and of course she has a cool hat and scarf. Today was the first day of radiation—she'll do 5 days a week for 6 weeks—it's only 10 minutes from our house and takes less than 10 minutes of treatment.

As mentioned before, they'll do the first MRI to see if any of this pesky business has come back in 2-3 months after the radiation treatment ends.

On Monday radiation treatments, we meet with the Dr. This morning, he was kind enough to say that the entire tumor board that reviewed her case were all saying that Lucy will do "much better than the statistics you read about on-line" . . . this made our day and of course we have felt this all the time.

Spirits are good and Lucy is continuing to walk each day and is getting near to the end of the park and hopes to get back her full distance in a couple of weeks. Keely has been so helpful and we could not be doing this patient/care giver/work thing without her love and support. Kyle continues to supply us with a Lb. of Starbucks each week (one of their perks) . . . we are very glad to have Kyle back from his auditions—good news, he has been accepted in the MFA program at CalArts (California Institute of the Arts) in Valencia, CA—he'll start this fall and is very excited and of course we are very proud.

2 weeks from daylight savings time—the sunshine has never felt better and we again, send our deepest thanks for all of your expressions and thoughts of support.

Love, Lucy, Tom, Keely and Kyle

March 15, 2009 Update
Spring Is One Week Away

Hi everyone

Lucy is feeling fine and is tolerating both the chemo and radiation very well—her hair is starting to fall out so she had one of Kyle's friends who is a stylist come over and give her a summer cut—more to follow if necessary. Nancy a neighbor living in Malaysia is here for a month to help out and has been taking Lucy to radiation so that I can keep working. Last weekend Barry and Shellie visited from Albuquerque and we had a very nice time—Barry and Shellie are Kyle's god parents and longtime friends from Billings. Her sister Shirley is here now and brother Tim is coming on Tuesday for a Reynolds St Patrick's day dinner. Lucy is still walking each day and has a couple of naps too—she will be on the radiation for 3 more weeks and continues the chemo—the chemo will be doubled after her radiation is done—her last blood works came up just fine so the chemo is being tolerated nicely so far. We appreciate all of the expressions of love and support—we continue to be home bodies and appreciate your patience with us as we tend to hunker down at home and not really get out a lot—who knows, we may have to have a Friday at Four with Spring around the corner—Keely is our personal landscape/gardener and our spinach has sprouted and the garlic looks great—Kyle starts rehearsals as Cowboy #1 in Oklahoma—the show opens in late May and runs through the end of June—we are excited because my mom is coming to visit then along with my sister Lee from Idaho—my sister Betty here in Denver has been keeping us pumped with her Master Gardner hints and tips for spring planting. Well enough for now—lots of thanks and love from Lucy Tom Keely and Kyle!

CHAPTER 15

MANY VISITORS AND TREATMENT SUGGESTIONS

One of the unexpected benefits of the neighborhood version of meals on wheels was that it gave our local friends and family an easy way to engage with us. Some, however, wanted to visit in person. These visits were always a wonderful expression of support and love, but it wasn't long before I had learned that I needed to play traffic cop/gate keeper and that I needed to do it in a sensitive, yet pragmatic, way.

Shortly after Lucy's surgery, out-of-town family and friends started asking when they could come and visit. I used the same gentle, yet firm traffic cop approach that I had used with the local folks, and I was careful to pace the visits so that Lucy had plenty of time to rest both during and after her treatments. Thankfully, all of the out of town visitors were very respectful of Lucy and her need for rest. I really never had to recite Lucy's mom's saying about family visits, "Fish and relatives both start to smell after three days," to any of our out-of-town visitors.

The visits from friends and family were not only therapeutic for Lucy, but also for Keely, Kyle, and me. For one thing, they gave me the opportunity to take breaks from my constant hovering over Lucy and her every move. I would often go for a bike ride or walk depending on the weather, finish some work that I had put off, or go have lunch with one of my buddies. I was able to get some "Tom time," which helped me keep my sanity and balance.

The visits also helped Lucy and I let off some steam. For example, Lucy's dear friends Kathleen and Phoebe (who, together with Lucy, had been known as the Tall, Tight, and Tan Sisters back in Billings) came down from Montana. They stayed with us, and we had one of Lucy's famous dinner parties—great food, great music, wine, and even some of Lucy's medical marijuana for those with such an interest.

Nights like this helped us forget Lucy's diagnosis for a few hours and reminded us what it was to have fun.

During their visits, some of our friends and family suggested certain ideas for fighting the cancer, including various diets and other lifestyle changes. While their hearts were in the right place, we decided to make decisions based on what our medical caregivers were saying as well as our personal feelings about a particular treatment. The great thing was that we felt no judgment from anyone.

Our oncology radiologist, who was fighting his own battle with cancer, did give us some suggestions for herbs and spices that may help, such as flaxseed and turmeric. We used these at times during the journey, mostly as spices in salads, rice dishes, and chicken meals. Flaxseed and its oil have long been used as food and dietary supplements with anti-cancer properties—it is an omega-3 fatty acid which some studies show suppresses the formation and growth of some types of cancers. Turmeric has an active ingredient that is an anti-oxidant which some believe prevents and slows the growth of different types of cancer.

Since neither we, nor the medical professionals really knew the cause of this type of brain cancer, we did what we could to get through each day, one day at a time.

April 19, 2009 Update
Radiation Is Done!

>   *Hi everyone—it's been a while since my last update—I am feeling really good—I finished the 7 weeks of radiation treatments on April 10th and am still napping but not as much—we went to the oncologist on Thursday and he is putting me on monthly chemo cycles which means I'll be continuing with the chemo but not the daily dose I took during*

radiation—the cycles will be five days of taking the chemo for every 28 days over the next 3-4 months—they bump up the dosage for these 5 days I take it. Oh I forgot the biggest news: I am now driving again—the Neurologist cleared me for driving the car and this has given me a great bump in positive energy! Another thing that lighted up my day was my cousin Cindi and her husband bringing by a framed poster celebrating the Obama inauguration—it is so cool. I have signed up with the National Brain Tumor Society for a Brain Tumor walk to be held in Denver on June 6th—it would be great for the locals to join me and our family for this walk—it's a fund raiser for the NBTS so if you wish you can donate; however, I'd just like it if you can join us—here's the link to sign up for Lucy' BT Team (I named the team and forgot the s after Lucy and can't figure out how to edit it. So that's the name)

Tom's brother Paul has an embroidery shop and we are planning on team tee shirts so if you like one, just get me your size. You may have heard me use the phase, talk, tight and tan . . . well the babes in the picture are the ones that inspired this phrase—this week Kathleen and Phoebe came down from Billings for a visit—we had a wonderful time—it's always a treat to see them and Phoebe seems to excel at finding kitchen magnets with a real message or two—when you are over next, be sure to check them out, I especially like the "Trailer Park" one. My sister Shirley is back for a visit and says that I look thinner, more alert and much fresher. Keely, Kyle and Tom are doing well—Keely has taken charge of the landscaping duties fresh with a new pole saw and other tools—she is just like me though, that is, she cuts things down and waits for Tom to do the clean up! We went to a Garden Show yesterday that Aunt Betty (Tom's sis) was working and stocked up on some cool plants—Betty introduced us to the woman who does the Rocky Mountain section for Sunset Magazine and we got some good free advice. Kyle is all set for CalArts and continues being a barista and keeping us hip with the latest Netflix. Tom is starting to lose some weight since we asked that folks not bring dinners; he is even getting back on his travel schedule.

You all have given me a new sense of being and it's all so good—never in my life have I felt as loved as I have since this thing started—guys, you make my day each and every day and I can't thank you enough—when the weather gets a little more reliable, I am planning a Friday at 4 to celebrate with all of you. For now, thanks for everything you have done and we'll connect sooner than later. Much Love, Lucy

CHAPTER 16

LUCY THE PERSON, THE HEALER

I would be remiss if I didn't share more about Lucy the person, not just Lucy the brain cancer patient.

Back when she was a pre-teen, Lucy and her family started going to Swan Lake in northwestern Montana for their two week summer vacation. Every year, they rented the same cabin and spent their time fishing and water skiing and making friends with other regulars at the lake.

Lucy fell in love with Montana during those vacations, and her college dream was to enroll at the University of Montana in Missoula, several hours from her beloved Swan Lake. Her parents wanted Lucy to be serious about college and insisted that she attend the University of Utah as a freshman, but they said that if she still wanted to go to Missoula after her freshman year, she would be free to go provided she paid some of the expenses.

Lucy completed her first year at the University of Utah and, using the money she earned working as a summer pool manager for Salt Lake County, enrolled at the University of Montana in the fall of 1972. She joined the Kappa Alpha Theta sorority where I bussed tables and did general kitchen work as a house boy. Of course, I met her immediately and tried to ask her out on a date, but later found out that she was engaged to a medical student at the University of Utah.

In the spring of 1974, I found out that Lucy's engagement was just a rumor she had put out so that she wouldn't have to initially deal with those pesky Montana boys looking for some out-of-state babe to date. We started dating and were married a year later. She was not the first Lucy Stockburger—my paternal grandmother had been named Lucy Stockburger.

Lucy and I always wanted children. Her first two pregnancies sadly ended with miscarriages, and we both went through extensive tests to determine a cause, but none was found. Lucy would never give up, though, and six years after were married, Keely was born. I will never forget Lucy's comment when the doctor handed Keely to her, and she held her for the first time. "Keely, you can't know how happy I am to see you!" Lucy said, a comment that reflected her joy that this pregnancy, at least, had ended in the best way possible.

Kyle was born four years later, and our family was complete. Lucy loved being a mom, especially a stay-at-home mom. Lucy's own mom had been a business person, and Lucy had had a nanny for most of her childhood and didn't want that for her kids.

Fast forward to our life in south Denver. Lucy had always been interested in health and fitness and decided to become a massage therapist. She chose the massage therapy profession largely because of her interest in healing. At the same time, it afforded her the opportunity to be a stay-at-home mom which was very important to her. In 1993, she enrolled in one of the best massage therapy colleges in the US, and for 14 months, she commuted daily to Boulder from Littleton—a round trip of over 100 miles. She graduated at the top of her class with straight A's and did her internship massaging dancers from the leading ballet company in Colorado.

Over her fifteen years as a certified massage therapist, Lucy developed a referral-only client list that expanded to well over 100 people. Her specialty was athletic injuries and other muscle aliments that could not be healed by traditional physical therapy, orthopedic surgery, chiropractic treatments, or prescribed pain or relaxation medicine. For the majority of her clients, Lucy used deep tissue or neuromuscular massage—or, as many called it, Lucy's House of Pain!

Through her practice, Lucy created a professional and personal bond with many of her clients. She not only helped heal her clients' aliments, but also took the time to be a good listener. It wasn't uncommon for her clients to, as she would say, "they spill their guts about everything from relationship issues to parenting problems." Of course, she was careful to keep what was said in the massage room, in the massage room. As a result, the lion's share of the folks on Lucy's friends and family email list included many of her clients.

Throughout her time as a massage therapist, Lucy stuck to massage therapy fundamentals. Though she could read and fluff people's auras, she shied away from what she called the "woo woo" treatments and kept up with the latest innovations by taking many continuing education classes.

During her fight with the cancer, Lucy received regular massages from her own massage therapist of 14 years. Lucy brought all of her collective healing experience to her fight with cancer. She studied, read new developments, and though she knew deep down that the odds were not in her favor, she maintained a positive attitude up until her death.

CHAPTER 17

O ne of the things I learned about being a caregiver to Lucy was that she coped with cancer much like the way she coped with any other adversity in her life. While some cancer patients become evangelists and crusaders in a very vocal and visible manner, this would have been out of character for Lucy. She was never one to bring attention to herself when she was dealing with tough issues in her life.

Some of our friends and family suggested activities to help her cope with the cancer. As with their recommendations about herbs and alternative treatments, they made these suggestions with the best of intentions, but those closest to Lucy knew that she would deal with this in her own way.

Lucy did act on some of their suggestions with the hope that by doing so, she would give strength to others, but even then it was out of character. For example, she decided to participate in and invite friends and family to join her at the annual Brain Tumor Association Walk in the spring of 2009. She asked my brother to print some cool tee shirts for all the members of Team Lucy, and he and his wife drove 600 miles from Montana so that they could hand deliver the tee shirts and walk with us. When we all got to the park the morning of the walk, Lucy grew very quiet. She did not want any of us to make a big deal about being there to support her, and she especially didn't want anyone bringing attention to her and Team Lucy.

My daughter later told me that she thought the reason why her mom had turned quiet at the walk was because that was the first time that she had come in face-to-face contact with other brain cancer patients. These patients were at various stages of their illness, and many were in wheel chairs or using walkers. The sight of them would have given Lucy a first-hand look at what was to come.

In the hopes of helping us cope with the reality of Lucy's cancer, Lucy and I went to a group therapy session sponsored by the hospital. There were several other cancer patients in attendance and after they told their stories, Lucy felt a deep empathy for them. She felt the great pain and anguish they were experiencing. This was the first and last group therapy session we attended because, as said before, Lucy did not want to burden others with her situation, and to do so would have been out of character. Lucy always had that "hunker down" mentality; once she knew the score, she got into her own survival mode, the mode that had helped her get through other tough times in her life. She did not want the rest of us to be burdened by her condition and did her best to bear the burden of her cancer by herself.

During that first year, I am sure that time passed differently for Lucy, the patient, than it did for the rest of us. Even though there were many long nights spent awake thinking about the inevitability of this type of cancer, time seemed to go by very quickly during the first year. We were in sprint mode, trying to do as much as we could, as quickly as we could. Everything you ever hear about fighting cancer successfully concerns early detection and fast action. As such, this sprint took us through the surgery, radiation, and chemotherapy in no time at all.

During this time, we talked about getting the necessary legal documents in place, including her living will/healthcare power of attorney and the durable power of attorney. True to form, Lucy took charge and used a respected online firm to complete both of these documents exactly as she wanted.

Lucy didn't talk much about what she was feeling inside during the treatment period; it was like she was in a zone that was focused solely on getting up each day and doing everything the physicians suggested.

During our marriage, Lucy always used laughter and good natured joking to relieve stress and tension. She brought this same approach to her cancer treatments. This not only helped her relieve stress and tension but it also helped her bond with her professional caregivers, from the receptionist in the surgeon's office to the entire staff at the oncologist's office.

All of her professional caregivers knew Lucy in a way that was more personal than their relationships with other patients. At least that was how it appeared. But, whether or not the connections were real, the way Lucy handled her interactions with the professional caregivers was a real lift for me and for her other caregivers—Lucy's good attitude made the otherwise stressful situation a little easier.

We all joked that each appointment would be 50% shorter if Lucy just allowed the doctor do the exam, asked some questions, and then moved on to the next thing. But, Lucy wasn't like other patients. She took the time to make these people feel her appreciation for what they were doing. On the last day of Lucy's first radiation treatment regimen, she brought the office bagels and cream cheese, and for her radiology technicians, she brought Bloody Mary mix and little bottles of vodka.

Another example of Lucy's levity was when our oncologist's internist handled the lengthy and required disclosure session regarding the potential side effects of the chemotherapy drug.

First of all, the internist was very attractive, young and outgoing. Lucy was quick to tell her that "Tom has no money," which she believed would keep me from flirting too much.

"No problem," the internist replied. "I'm happily married to an older man, and my kids keep us both very busy when I'm not at my day job."

When the internist got to the part about the high toxicity of the chemo drug, she said that we could only handle the pills with surgical gloves that Lucy was to flush the toilet twice after peeing, that we had to be sure to use condoms during intercourse, and that Lucy had to avoid oral sex. The internist paused after the oral sex comment and said, "bummer." We all laughed.

June 28, 2009 Update
Wow, It's Almost July!

> *Hi everyone—apologies for not providing an update*
> *sooner—I'd like to thank those that came to the Brain*

Tumor Walk on June 6th and of course those that donated and were unable to attend—I didn't quite make the 3 mile walk around Sloan's Lake but did really enjoy seeing those that came—Tom's bother Paul and his wife Carla from Billings brought down some cool tee shirts with a fighting hummingbird logo so Team Lucy looked good and as you know I have always like to have the team look good! The weekend was good with Tom's mom, 2 sisters and brother in town. We all went and saw Kyle in Oklahoma on Saturday night and of course his performance was great and it was nice that more of the family got to see him in a show—everyone was raving about Keely's magic touch with the garden—they also got to meet Keely's Jakester and his parents—special thanks to Jake's parents Roxanne and John along with his sister-in-law Nicole for walking. The yard, flowers and garden have never looked better thanks to Keely—the beauty helps me through each day. Tom's sister, Betty, has kept us in good supply of tomato plants and with this last week's heat and sun, they are looking good—Tom harvested the first batch of garlic and planted the basil this week—I've even learned to stomach the aroma of fish emulsion from fertilizing the garden! Thursday I finished my 3rd chemo cycle (5 days of the heavy dose of chemo drug)—I am really glad that I will have 23 days off—right now our oncologist has the 4th and final cycle scheduled to begin on July 19th. My last blood work came up fine and other than still being tired and having come lingering nausea, I am doing just fine although I am not a real ball of fire these days (still napping a lot) and look forward to feeling better each day—our Radiologist says it takes 3-6 months to get over the side effects of the radiation and am I ready! The next big day is July 9th when I'll have my first MRI since the radiation—it may be inconclusive but we are ready for whatever the outcome and we all are still very optimistic that the cancer has not come back. Tom and I talk a lot these days to keep us both sane while we wait for the MRI—with Keely and Kyle's help, Tom is able to keep working—he even got on an airplane once in the past 6 months. No big plans for the summer but I am hopeful that as I feel better, we'll be able to get out more and to the mountains which I really miss—we are planning on going to Missoula for homecoming and to celebrate my sorority's 100th anniversary—some of my pals from Theta called Friday night and it was good to hear from them. Again many thanks for all of your expressions of love and support—you have all contributed to my good spirits in oh so many ways and I will never be able to fully express my love and appreciation—I'll look forward to letting you know how the next 3 weeks goes and won't be as tardy with my updates. Love to you all and thanks for everything you do, Lucy

July 16, 2009 Update
Some Encouraging News

On Thursday July 16th, we received good news that the tumor area did not show any signs of growth—this good news was overshadowed two days later when our dog Sadie died suddenly. Sadie was only five years old and Lucy's best buddy.

Hi everyone! It's been quite a week. I had my MRI last Thursday—our oncologist had the Neurosurgeon and Radiologist review the MRI and they all talked before we got the update. The net is that I am feeling very good, the MRI results are encouraging and I will be getting another MRI on August 20th to get a more definitive read on the results. The MRI showed no evidence of recurrence or tissue damage which is good news; however there were some "cloudy" areas adjacent to where the tumor was removed and the next MRI should give us more on the cloudy areas. My last blood work came up fine and other than my platelet's being a little lower—I go back in on Monday for another CBC before I start my 4th and last chemotherapy cycle. During the time between having the MRI and getting the results we had a major upset. Our dog Sadie died in her sleep suddenly. We woke up Saturday morning and Sadie was sleeping in her normal spot and when Tom went to get her rolling, he discovered that she was dead—there was no trauma or any indicators of being poisoned or anything—we think that she must have had a heart attack, stroke or some other type of sudden event. We'll miss her a lot; she was a great dog. Thanks again to everyone for your love support and prayers. Love, Lucy

CHAPTER 18

HELPING OUR ADULT CHILDREN COPE

Lucy and I talked often about how Keely and Kyle were coping with the brain cancer. Beginning with the initial diagnosis, we had decided that we did not want to sugarcoat anything. We felt that it was much better for the kids to understand the reality of the situation. Even so, we did not want to act like it was all doom and gloom, or that we had given up and were taking the prognosis lying down. Lucy had always been a fighter, and we did not want the kids to think that we were just going to sit back, do the treatments, and then wait for Lucy to eventually die.

This was tough stuff for our kids to handle, especially, as with many families, our kids had a very special relationship with Lucy—for example, they both preferred to talk to Lucy whenever there was something serious to discuss. In a certain sense, I was lucky that both of our kids were over 25 years old when Lucy was diagnosed. I have a friend, Joan, whose husband died of the same type of brain cancer ten years ago. Her daughters were only ten and eight years old at the time of his death, and I know that what she had to deal with her kids was much different than what I went through and am going through to this day. Still, loss is loss, no matter the age.

As might be expected, the cancer brought us all closer together as a family. It also caused each of us to put our day-to-day life issues and petty drama in perspective knowing that Lucy now had her biggest fish to fry—now it wasn't just a friend's mom, dad, brother, or sister who was fighting cancer.

It's always sad when someone else is diagnosed, but it's hard to really feel the pain on a personal level; however, when it hit our family, we all gained new perspectives, respect, and insights.

I am not sure if our kids ever surfed the internet about Lucy's type of cancer, but I was quick to let them know that if they did research GBM's on the internet, they should be prepared, because it was not all that encouraging. Finding a balance between letting Keely and Kyle know exactly what was going on and being optimistic and hopeful that Lucy would beat the statistics was really tough for us. There were times when each of our kids felt and expressed that they wanted me to be more optimistic because they thought that positive vibes and energy helped Lucy's fight with the cancer.

Since I was getting great value and support from my cancer counseling, I suggested that Keely and Kyle go as well. They did go to a session together, and I never did get all the details, but both felt that the counseling was just not what they wanted or needed at the time. I applauded them for trying, though. I think part of why it didn't work for them was that they were both already getting a lot of unsolicited advice about how to cope, and the session just pushed them over the edge. Also, I suspect they felt that, since I was already getting some help, the counselor was really mine and not theirs.

Lucy was worried about how all of us would cope, survive, and continue to live our lives without her. One thing that both Lucy and I remained steadfast about was our conviction that both kids continue on with their lives while we all fought the cancer.

Lucy was very happy that Keely had found Jake, the love of her life. Jake and Keely had been dating for two years when the cancer was diagnosed, and he was a huge help during that tough time. The first time Keely brought Jake home, Lucy told me, "Keely is going to marry Jake," and two years later he did, with my blessing—Lucy had long ago let Keely know that she approved of Jake.

Kyle was a different story. Based on his grad school auditions in New York, Kyle was accepted into a three-year master's program at one of the most innovative and demanding fine arts schools in the world. The school was located 40 minutes north of Los Angeles. The fact that Kyle's graduate program was so demanding really helped him because it meant that he didn't have a lot of free time to dwell. Even so, I am certain that it was not easy for Kyle being in Southern California while Keely and I did front line duty with Lucy.

August 20, 2009 Update
Very Good News Today

    Hi all—first of all thank you for your expressions of support, thoughts and prayers over the past months! Whew! My MRI this morning showed that things have 'stabilized' which according to the Neurosurgeon is very good news—no evidence of recurrence of the cancer and the 'cloudy area' from the previous MRI has not changed—we meet with the oncologist on Monday for more details; the net is that we are breathing a huge sigh of relief. I'll have another MRI in 3 months and am sure that these will continue with the interim begin expanded. I am looking forward to going back to work in September and told Kyle that it's okay for him to start graduate school in 2 weeks (he was going anyway but this makes it easier) and it's okay for [1]Keely to move from being nurse to student or whatever she is thinking. Tom may even get back on an airplane for work! I have never experienced such warmth and support from friends and family as experienced with you—I will always cherish your support and caring—you guys rock! A very, very, very big thank you from Lucy, Tom, Keely and Kyle.

CHAPTER 19

A RETURN TO NORMALCY

With the continuous good news, Lucy and I tried to get our lives back to normal. We both knew that it was a new normal, though, and neither of us put our heads in the sand when it came to the odds of beating the cancer.

We talked about the importance of at least trying to get back to our regular life so that Keely, Kyle, our family, and our friends would see that we were not giving up hope—keeping a positive attitude really helped us all cope.

We held some of our dinner parties on Fridays. We started the evenings at 4:00 PM, and Lucy would last as long as she could before quietly sneaking off to bed, although she wasn't really sneaking, as many of us had our eyes on her. However, we were careful not to let on that we were watching. Lucy was always sensitive that people would be looking at her, thinking that they were looking for some sign of the cancer beyond the hairless side of her head where the tumor had been removed—other than that, it was hard to tell by looking that Lucy had any illness. After Lucy had gone to bed, the parties would carry on as they had before with Tom's new music, fun, and good times.

Within several months of our dog Sadie dying, Lucy and Keely decided to get a puppy. Lucy reminded me that we had owned a dog during most of our time together, so this was part of what "normal" meant for us. She also thought it would be a really good thing for Keely to help her pick out a puppy.

Keely and Lucy come home one sunny afternoon with Uma, our new, black, Scotty puppy.

Later Lucy confided in me that she got Uma in part because she knew that I would really need a buddy when she was gone. Once again, Lucy was right. Every day since Lucy died, Uma has gotten me up, saying with her doggie eyes, "Time for our walk." Uma now insists on an early morning and an early evening walk each day.

In October, Lucy, accompanied by her friend, Char, took a long weekend trip to Seattle to visit Lucy's sister, Shirley. They wore their matching "peace sign" bathrobes and brought one for Shirley. They even braved Shirley's driving and spent several days on the Oregon coast at Cannon Beach. Lucy slept most of the time, but it was very beneficial for her spirits to know that she could still get on an airplane and take a trip.

Cannon Beach, Shirley, Lucy and Char

November 13, 2009 Update
MRI Results

> Hi everyone—I had my 3 month MRI this morning and just got the preliminary results from the PA in the neurosurgeon's office—everything is stable with no signs of recurrence—we are breathing a lot easier—they are talking about the next MRI being in 6 months but I won't know until I see our oncologist next Friday—all is well here in Denver—winter has already struck with about 2 feet of snow a couple of weeks ago—of course it was 71 yesterday and a new storm is on its way. Thanks for all the continued love, prayers and support—will hopefully keep in better touch—my love to you all, Lucy

CHAPTER 20

For the next nine months, we did not send out any email updates. Instead, we took the "no news is good news" approach, though we did keep in contact with individuals via phone calls and the occasional personal email. Frankly, I think our friends and family welcomed the break as much as we did.

During this period, we tried to get back to as normal life as possible. Lucy started her walks again and resumed driving and doing her normal day-to-day activities with multiple naps to help her continued recovery from the surgery, radiation, and chemotherapy. But, Lucy could not resume all of her normal activities. Lucy's massage therapist days were over, and that hurt her because she had truly enjoyed the work and interactions with her many clients. She referred all of her clients to her massage therapist of 15 years, Helen. Lucy had been Helen's massage therapist as well. Helen was one of the conduits for Lucy updates to her former clients.

In early January 2010, Lucy came with me on a business trip to San Diego. It was a conference with very flexible hours, so Lucy and I were able to have some quality time alone, relaxing at a resort. The warmer weather in San Diego was a nice break from the cold of the Rocky Mountains. While in California, we drove up to see Kyle and his school. Visiting him was very important to all of us, especially Lucy.

Whenever I traveled for work, I always made sure that someone stayed with Lucy, whether it was Keely or one of Lucy's many friends who volunteered to help.

CHAPTER 21

TEASING OURSELVES AND PERHAPS A BARGAIN

With the continued positive news about the tumor area being stable, we were able to get on with our lives from the standpoint of making some plans.

I think it is fair to say that neither Lucy nor I felt we were out of the woods as far as beating the odds of this type of cancer. Both of us had read enough about this type of cancer to know that the statistics were not in our favor. Having said this, there was a sense of hope that all of us were feeling.

We let ourselves hope, and in a sense be teased, by the fact that the GBM was encapsulated, by the oncologist's words that Lucy was a miracle, by the tests that over the past months showed no growth, and by all of our friends and family who put positive spins on anything they could, including Lucy's chance of survival. In any case, there was an atmosphere that we had turned the corner, and we needed to try and get back to a *normal* life.

When Lucy was initially diagnosed with the cancer, I suggested that we sell everything and travel, checking off everything left on Lucy's bucket list. Lucy had quickly brought me back to reality by saying that was a stupid idea and that even if we sold everything; we probably couldn't afford to travel anyway. She simply said that she had lived the life she wanted and felt she was the luckiest person in the world to have done what she wanted, when she wanted. "My bucket list has been checked off," she said with all sincerity.

She reminded me that she had always lived in the moment and that we as a family had traveled and experienced life to the fullest. This would end up being one of the topics that helped her get through until the end, and it was her way of letting me and our kids know that she was very happy to have lived a full life.

25 years into our marriage, Lucy confided in me about some terrible things that she had experienced as a child. I will not share the details because they were only Lucy's to share. Looking back on Lucy's optimism during this time, I had the feeling that Lucy had made some type of bargain with her God that involved being allowed to survive in return for the terrible things she had experienced as a child.

I knew that this *bargain* was over when Lucy asked me to watch a video of a news interview with the doctor treating Senator Ted Kennedy's brain cancer. When asked why he was so focused on brain cancer, the doctor, an internationally renowned neuro-oncolocgist, said something like, while the symptoms of other types of cancer are more horrific than brain cancer, most of those types of cancer can be cured, but there is no cure for brain cancer—it kills.

CHAPTER 22

E ven with the positive news that there had been no recurrence of the cancer and our return back to a normal life, the stress of the previous year was catching up with us.

The economy had not improved, I had a new boss who was turning up the heat to make the next big sale, our finances were paycheck to paycheck, and my wife was dying.

Try as I might, I just could not shake the reality of Lucy's cancer. Her death from the disease was not a question of *if,* but *when.* Even though I held out hope for a miracle, my gut knew there was not going to be a happy ending.

My way of coping was based on the following:

- My continued belief that each moment I got with Lucy following the seizure was a blessing.
- My commitment to Lucy and our children to do the best job I could possibly do as her primary caregiver—doing anything less was not an option. In essence, this meant being a good role model.
- My belief that, while I couldn't control the ultimate outcome, I could control my actions, attitude, and demeanor during the cancer, and that this would result in positive outcomes for the rest of my life
- By doing my best to care for Lucy, I felt this would mitigate any feelings of guilt that I may have about not doing more for her care.
- The comparison of my continued support of Lucy to winning a long, complex sales deal. During an especially tough deal, I had to hunker down and do whatever was

necessary to convince the potential new customer that my solution and commitment would result in their success. If I handled the situation correctly, it would result in me beating my competition to earn the customer's trust and would result in a new sale. Supporting Lucy through the cancer was the most important sales deal of my life!

- The commencement of the grieving process. My cancer counselor was helpful at each stage of the cancer fight—she always said a miracle was possible, but she was also quick to remind me of the realities of this type of cancer. This helped me mange my expectations and, in a certain way, gave me permission to begin my grieving.

- The wonderful outpouring of love and support from friends and family. During this time, I saw the true character of people. In spite of all the hate, bigotry, and intolerance in the world, Lucy's world was filled with love from some very different and unique people.

- My ability to stay employed. I was actually able to sell some software and make new customers during this time. Knowing I had the skills to sell while dealing with personal adversity was comforting.

- Having the opportunity to blow off some steam in a safe and non-judgmental environment—for example, when Kathleen and Phoebe came down in March, we were able to laugh and party much like we had done over the years in Billings.

- The chance to travel with Lucy. The San Diego trip in early January gave both of us a much needed break, as did our return to San Diego in June for a dear friend's daughter's wedding and a surprise birthday party.

- Prayer, faith, and a belief in miracles. While my faith in organized religion had declined, I continued to believe in a higher being and life after death.

More than anything, my attitude and basic work ethic helped me cope. These had been shaped by people who had taught me the difference between right and wrong, as well as the importance of putting in an honest day's work, loving thy neighbor as thyself, treating everyone with respect, owning up to your mistakes, and being loved and accepted by the love of my life, Lucy. Lucy's courage and passion for life set an example that gave me little or no room for doing anything other than being my best.

August 24, 2010 Update
The 2nd Surgery

Lucy's three month MRI in August 2010 showed an enhancement near the area where the first tumor had been removed. The members of Lucy's medical team—the oncologist, the neurosurgeon, and the neurologist—all agreed that this enhancement should come out as soon as possible.

At this point, we hadn't sent out an update to Lucy's friends and family network since the previous November, although most of them had kept in touch via phone and email. With this in mind, we re-started the updates, as it was the easiest and quickest way to keep everyone current with what was happening.

> *Hi everyone—hope all is well with you and your families—I know I have talked with some of you already, but wanted to let all know that my 3 month MRI last week showed an "enhancement" adjacent to where the first tumor was removed—our oncologist, Radiologist and Neurosurgeon all concur that it should come out—so this Friday, I go back in for brain surgery to remove the matter. I should be home Monday.*
>
> *Tom and I met with the Neurosurgeon today and saw the MRI—the "enhancement" is about a third of the size of the previous tumor and in a very safe place to remove—should be no side effects other than potential loss of some peripheral vision—Tom will send out an update sometime late Friday to let you know how surgery went.*
>
> *It looks like no more full radiation, but there are some options if it comes back again including another surgery and/or the cyber or gamma knife which is much focused radiation—perhaps some chemo.*

I know that all of your support has helped me and our family get through the first round and I appreciate your thoughts, prayers and any good vibes being sent our way.

We remain very optimistic and as you know, I am so ornery that I am not going anywhere without the strongest and hardest fight which you guys have helped me with before.

Look for updates from Tom—I love you all and appreciate the continued support.

Love, Lucy

August 27, 2010 Update
Lucy's Surgery Status

Good afternoon everyone—Lucy has come through the surgery with flying colors—they let me in recovery and she was cracking wise . . . a big surprise, yeah right! We later spent some brief time with her in ICU and she is very coherent and again cracking jokes.

The Neurosurgeon said that the tiny tumor looks like a "progression" from the previous one but that they will wait for CU Med school to weigh in which may take 4-5 days. He said based on how well Lucy did in surgery, she may be able to go home on Sunday; of course we will not push that since she gets such great care.

Special thanks to our Knoll's family—when Lucy and I turned the last corner to leave the neighborhood at 6:45am this morning, we were greeted by friends standing on the corner with hearts taped on, surgical masks and the like—of course there were even wine glasses to toast Lucy—what such great friends to have such a thoughtful send off! Thanks to Linda, Nancy and all for organizing—Lucy was blown away as were Keely and Kyle. We'll send a picture when we get one.

Thank you all for your expressions of love and support—I'll be sure to keep you posted on her progress—love to all and thank you, Tom, Keely and Kyle

Knolls Neighborhood Send-off

August 28, 2010 Update
Lucy Out of the ICU

Good afternoon everyone—Lucy is doing fine today—she was moved out of the ICU after lunch today and very likely will come home on Sunday. The incision was sutured rather than staples and they took off the head dressing—Lucy is glad to be on the 4th floor because it is so quite—she has been walking and is really only hooked up to the device that measures oxygen.

No news from the Neurosurgeon other than he feels she is doing so good that she can come home on Sunday. We all appreciate the expressions of support and love—it is so nice to have such good friends. She has her appetite back—Keely, Kyle and Jake (Keely's boyfriend) brought her Wendy's today. Her sister Shirley and I were there later until she kicked us out so she could get some rest.

They did an MRI this morning and I am sure we'll get a read from the Dr. about how clean the resection was when he makes rounds.

Not out of the woods with this nasty stuff, but definitely on the road to recovery from surgery—I just can't believe that she had brain surgery yesterday and spent only 1 day in ICU—but of course, as we know Lucy, she is very strong.

That's all for now, but did want to let you all know that she sends her love and is doing great.

Much love, Tom, Keely and Kyle

August 29, 2010 Update
Lucy's Home

Hi everyone—Lucy got home about 1:30pm today and is doing great—I knew she really wanted to come home when she called me this morning at 7:00AM to let me know she had showered and was dressed—we had a nice breakfast and waited for the Dr. to release her.

According to the Dr. the MRI looks like they got the tumor and a good perimeter. She is pretty tired but I am just amazed how alert and more full of energy this time. I will be taking full advantage of me being able to boss her around and will be sure that she gets plenty of rest; this may last only a few days as you know, I rarely get to be bossy, or at least if I try it really has little impact.

We really appreciate all of your continued love, prayers and warm expressions of support including some great meals—Kyle is worried because he was trying to lose a pound or two before heading back to school. Shirley leaves this evening and we have really appreciated her being here.

I am taking some days off, Kyle stays until Wednesday and Keely is taking Thursday and Friday off to be close—again thanks for the help—chat soon—Love, Tom Keely and Kyle

CHAPTER 23

Meeting with my cancer counselor provided a safe place for me to ask hard questions away from Lucy, friends, and family. These were questions that I needed to have answered, but couldn't ask in front of Lucy and the doctors. Some of the things I asked about included questions such as, "Is it normal to start to think about life as a single person? Is it normal to start to think about dating? What should I do if my children don't want to go through Lucy's personal belongings when I feel it is time? Should I immediately put the house up for sale and plan my move home to Montana? When will I know when it's time for hospice? What will death be like for Lucy? Will it be painful for her?"

I started to think about whom I would hang out with when Lucy was gone. I have always been better friends with women than with men, and this scared me because I really did not have many close male friends. During our marriage, I hadn't had fishing or golfing buddies—after a busy work week, I usually just wanted to be with Lucy and the kids.

Lucy and I did talk some about my life after she was gone. She was adamant about supporting the kids, but in a way that didn't get in their way from being on their own. She told me many times, especially during the last months, that she felt blessed to have had such a wonderful life with me. Even though we were financially strapped, Lucy always let me know that she traveled as much as she wanted and had done the things that she wanted to do and had no regrets.

We often talked about some of our best times together, such as going to our first US Tennis Open, the many trips to Maui, and the trip to Italy. When we became empty nesters, Lucy would always say, "As much as I love my children, it is nice to be back as we started—as a couple."

Lucy had massage clients who were attractive, single women several years younger than me. Of course I had noticed them over the years, and frankly, my thoughts during this time did start to wander to thinking about what would happen if I got together with one of them after Lucy died.

It was especially difficult when some of these attractive, single women would say to me, "Is there anything I can do for you, Tom? Really, anything?" I often just wanted to reply, "How about a big hug and a kiss?" While Lucy and I were more intimate during her cancer than at any other time in our marriage, I did miss the sex and started thinking about how I was going to handle this part of my life after she was gone.

While Lucy had the greatest respect for these attractive, single women, she urged me to avoid chasing after the trust fund babies and country club girls who had come from some type of wealth and a different level on the socioeconomic scale. She warned me by saying, "They will eat you alive!"

I asked her what she meant by this. She just laughed and said again, "They will eat you alive!"

Once again, Lucy was right. Since Lucy's death, I have dated several women from different levels of the socioeconomic scale, and each time, I was eaten alive. I believe Lucy knew I had too big of a heart and would care too much. I think this was why, every time one of these women came to visit during her cancer, Lucy would always say, "Remember, Tom has no money!"

Doing "what ifs" was part of my grieving process and helped me get ready for the next chapter in my life.

CHAPTER 24

This is the too much information (TMI) part that my kids and others close to us may want to skip. However, for potential caregivers, I feel a need to share my thoughts about what to do with your intimacy when your partner has cancer.

When the cancer was first diagnosed, Lucy and I had been together for 35 years. We essentially had grown up as adults together, and intimacy had always been a very important part of our relationship, even through the menopause years and as we approached 60.

We had always enjoyed a very active sex life together. There were times when it was all about her, and yes, times when it was all about me—but mostly it was all about both of us.

Throughout Lucy's fight with cancer, we kept our intimacy, but the sex part was essentially over from day one. Frankly, during most of the first year, sex was not on either of our radars, but towards the end of the first year and into the second, Lucy expressed some guilt about the fact that she was not up to sex. She knew how important sex had been for our level of intimacy, and so she offered on many occasions to, as she used to say, "take one for the team."

Taking one for the team was a very nice offer, and a typical example of Lucy worrying about others. However, it just did not feel right to me. I knew she was not the same Lucy as before, and it just wasn't the right thing to do. Usually by the time we were finished discussing this, we both had fallen asleep.

Each couple has to handle this part of cancer in a way that works best for them and their circumstances. I wanted to share my own experience because this is one area that the doctors usually don't talk about unless it comes up during discussions about side effects or chemotherapy drug precautions.

September 2010 Updates

September 10—Hi everyone—first of all thanks for all the expressions of support! The biopsy came back and a portion of the tumor that was removed had the stage 4 cancer back—not great news, but the surgeon feels that he got a very good perimeter around the tumor and this is good.

We meet with the oncologist first thing Monday morning to discuss next steps—I do know that I have another MRI scheduled in 3 months and am anxious to hear what our oncologist suggests.

More to follow—love you guys and thanks again for all the support!

Love, Lucy

September 17—Hi everyone—thanks so much for all of the love and support—I am headed back for chemo beginning on Sept 30th—it will be 2 drugs also may have a gamma knife (very focused radiation) to get a larger perimeter around where the 2nd tumor was removed—am a little scared as you would expect but am not going down without a very strong fight—back to walking getting ready for chemo and what's ahead.

Keely and Kyle are doing great and Tom, well he is hanging in as well.

Just a quick update to let you all know—we remain very optimistic and will keep in touch—my love to you all, Lucy

December 12, 2010 Update
Our Autumn Adventure

Hi everyone—apologies for not checking in sooner—I know that I have chatted with some of you but did want to share how things are going.

In mid-August, my regular MRI showed that the cancer had come back near the same area—on August 27th, I had my 2nd brain surgery and the cancer was removed—I recovered nicely in fact the surgery was on Friday and I was home Sunday. Over the next several months we were in a holding pattern—a MRI in the first week of November showed that the cancer had come back a 3rd time and I went in for a gamma knife treatment which is focused radiation which removed the cancer—this treatment was very non-invasive and I was home the same day.

I have been on a chemo regime which is 7 days taking the chemo and 14 days off—we timed this so I would be in my off cycle for Thanksgiving and Christmas.

I had a MRI last week and the results were every positive—no cancer and the gamma knife did a great job—my oncologist called me a miracle! I will be doing the chemo for another 2 months and will have MRI's on a 6 week schedule.

My spirits are good and you wouldn't know that I have cancer by looking at me—I am taking several naps a day and not getting out as much as I would like to since my immune system is not strong from the chemo.

Keely and Kyle are being strong and are a source of strength for me—we had a nice Thanksgiving and are looking forward to driving (weather permitting of course) to Billings for Christmas—Tom's mom is 86 and he has not been with his mom for Christmas for a long time—both Keely and Kyle are going as well as our dog, Uma. Tom is doing fine and he is looking forward to taking some time off.

All in all, I feel very blessed to be here and am really encouraged with the gamma knife treatment. Tom and I are back to watching some movies at home and just finished the mini-series Pillars of the Earth which was great.

Thanks for all of your continued support, love, good thoughts and prayers. The meals and other expressions of support are very much appreciated—it brings me great joy to feel your good vibes and I am sure that it has really made a difference in my ability to continue to fight.

All of my very best to you for the holidays—Keely, Kyle, Tom and I are so lucky to have such great friends and family.

Love to all, Lucy

CHAPTER 25

MY MELTDOWN

During most of 2010, the stress of the previous year built up until it finally started to catch up with me. While painful to discuss, I think it's important to mention this for the benefit of other future caregivers. Simply stated, I had started to self-medicate by drinking much more alcohol than I should have.

With the cancer back and with a new boss who was turning up the heat on my sales activities, I chose to numb myself at night. There were times when I drove when I shouldn't have and others when I was in no condition to get Lucy to a hospital if needed. I rationalized my drinking in many different ways; I told myself that I had been such a good caregiver the first year that I deserved some Tom time. In some sense, I felt that so much concern had been focused on Lucy that I wanted someone to be concerned about me.

My drinking was confined to the evenings only with an occasional beer on Saturday afternoon; fortunately, I never became a day drinker. Even so, I was no longer adhering to my original convictions that I stay clear-minded and able to care for Lucy at all times.

I discussed my drinking with my cancer counselor, and while understanding, she was quite clear that this was not the way to deal with the situation. However, I didn't change my ways until I absolutely had to. My wakeup call came from two different directions at about the same time.

First, my second new boss in five months tried to fire me shortly before Thanksgiving because I was not meeting my sales target. My first thought was, "how dare you try and fire me when I am right in the middle of helping my wife fight a terminal illness?" Losing my job would mean that I would also lose the low cost of our health insurance. As a result, our costs would increase from $150/month to over $1,500/month—yes, COBRA provides continued coverage, but at an extreme premium! Luckily, I was able to stave off being forced to quit or being fired by getting my boss's boss to intercede—although, it would be a short lived reprieve.

Second, my family and several close friends who had noticed my excessive drinking nicely suggested that I start using a shot glass to measure the gin in my gin and tonics. I knew that I was drinking too much at night and felt relieved when my others took the time and care to let me know their feelings. When I did start using a shot glass, I let them know that I could now taste the tonic part of the drink.

I changed my self-medicating primarily due to my family and friends' gentle intervention and because I once again wanted to be fully on my game for Lucy and work. I also felt that this change was especially important for my kids—how could I help them deal with their mother's terminal illness if I was off the deep end? They didn't need to have to worry about the both of us at the same time, though, I knew that there were times when they did worry about the both of us and how we were coping.

My father was an alcoholic, as was Lucy's mother and I should have known better, but at the time I just didn't have the awareness that I should have had.

As a caregiver it is important to take the best care of yourself, because otherwise, you won't be in any shape to help the ones you're supposed to be caring for. Once I realized this, I started taking our new puppy, Uma, for morning walks before my first cup of coffee and really revved up my reading to get some healthier Tom time.

CHAPTER 26

SENSING A DECLINE

Right before Christmas, Lucy decided to go to a spice store in downtown Littleton to get some gifts for her friends and her oncology radiologist. At this point, she had been driving off and on with no problems.

Not long after she left, I got a frantic phone call from Lucy. She had just bumped into a car and wanted to know if I could come down to help. Since she had the car, I called a neighbor for a ride. By the time I got there, the police had issued a citation and already gone. Fortunately the bump had really just been a minor tap. There were no damages to either car, and the person she had bumped into was fine.

Lucy was pretty shaken up, though. She had lost the peripheral vision in her left eye from the surgeries and just hadn't seen the car. She said, "What if that had been a mom pushing her child in a baby carriage? Tom, I am through driving."

Her choice took one more tough decision off of my plate. I was so proud of Lucy deciding this on her own. Again, she was demonstrating her selfless nature by giving up a piece of her independence so that she didn't accidentally cause harm to others.

Several weeks later, on a sunny Sunday afternoon in early January, we were sitting outside watching the snow melt. When she stood up to go inside, she started to shake, and I had to catch her to keep her from falling and then help her inside for her nap.

While Lucy was napping, I called the oncologist's office. I initially wondered if the shaking had been a result of her being in the sun for too long even though I had made her wear a hat, but the oncologist indicated that the shaking was likely a side effect of all of her treatments.

Later, I chatted with the cancer counselor about this, and she said that with all the surgeries, radiation, and chemotherapy drugs that I could expect various side effects and that this might well be one of them.

My cancer counselor suggested that now was the time for me to take full advantage of all of the kind offers friends and family had made to help care for Lucy. Heretofore, I had been reluctant to accept help when I could do things myself. But, as the cancer counselor said, "You have to be able to get some time to breath. Besides, people do want to help—even with little things like picking up takeout food or getting groceries or just coming over to chat with Lucy so you can get out and regenerate your energy."

From this point forward, I acted much like a first time parent with a toddler just beginning to walk. I entered helicopter mode and hovered around Lucy, watching for any indication that I might need to catch her and prevent her from falling and hurting herself.

I also started to check around the house to see what changes needed to be made to make the house safer and easier for Lucy to navigate. I had already put a mattress pad protector on the bed with comfortable sheets. Fortunately, our bedroom was on the main floor, so we did not need to do much in terms of adding safety items other than installing grab bars in the master bathroom.

CHAPTER 27

FULFILLING LAST WISHES

By the beginning of the last year of Lucy's cancer, I had started seeing signs of decline. Unsurprisingly, Lucy had also noticed them and had begun to talk about this being her last year.

We did not talk in any detail about her memorial service. Lucy was clear that she wanted to be cremated and that I should spread some of her ashes at the top of Paradise Divide near Crested Butte, Colorado. She also expressed a desire to have some be spread at Swan Lake in Montana, or at any other place I thought appropriate.

Lucy was adamant that any obituary I write not include anything like, "After a long and courageous battle with brain cancer, Lucy . . ." Again, she did not want to bring attention to herself or her death from cancer. I asked her if she wanted Catholic last rites to be performed, and she said yes. While Lucy was not a practicing Catholic, she had always had a deep faith in her God.

I am told that some couples dealing with cancer spend a lot of time discussing details, including end-of-life requests, what type of remembrance service would be held, what the obituary would say, and who gets what, etc. We did not. I never pressed Lucy about these matters because knowing Lucy as I did for over 37 years, I knew that if she wanted to discuss these topics, she would do so in her own way and time.

Lucy trusted me to do what I thought was best in these areas. Indeed, the funeral services were planned after she died and turned out to be much as Lucy would have expected—a non-traditional gathering, celebrating life and the life and love of Lucy. It was true to Lucy and the way she lived her life with the people who were important to her.

There were really only two things that Lucy wanted to do that she talked about repeatedly. First, she wanted to see Kyle in his lead role in a play called *Wounded* that would be performed at his graduate school in the last part of February. Next, she wanted to take one last summer trip with just the four of us to the Seeley Swan Valley in northwestern Montana.

January 15, 2011 Update

Good morning everyone—as always, thank you for all of the expressions of support—you really help me with this fight. I had my 6 week follow-up MRI this week and the results are inconclusive—there is some "enhancement" which could be either a progression of the cancer or healing from the treatments—our neurosurgeon, oncologist and radiologist all agree that we are in a wait and see mode and will scheduled the next MRI in 5 weeks.

I continue my chemo regime and start the 4th cycle on Monday—the chemo pretty much whacks me hard and I end up sleeping a lot during the 7 days on and then get a respite for the 2 weeks off—my attitude continues to be very positive and the cup is definitely half full.

Tom and the kids are hanging in there as best they can and are always keeping me on my toes with positive vibes. Kyle is back in school after being in a production in Mexico that CalArts has with a fine arts school in Guadalajara. He is getting ready for his lead role in a play called Wounded. It's a take-off on bury my heart at wounded knee and over the holiday break, he and Tom drove out to the Sand Creek massacre national site just east of here (Tom is finally using his Anthropology degree!). Keely is keeping the City of Lakewood alive and well with her landscaping job and has begun some spring planting in their greenhouse. Tom has to go to his company kick-off meeting this week and Keely is staying with me which is great.

We are planning a snow shoe picnic in a couple of weeks to celebrate Tom's last birthday as a fifty year old—it's tough being the trophy wife to such an older guy!

When we lived in Montana, we always joked that "January is the longest 2 months of the years" and yet this year it is going way too fast; however my friends and family in Montana are telling me that it really is a long January with snow and cold.

My spirits are good thanks to all of your love, support and prayers. Thanks to all and with much love, Lucy

February 2, 2011 Update
No More "Wait and See"

Hi everyone—it has been quite a ride over the past several weeks—2 weeks ago, Lucy's Neurologist and Radiologist suggested that we consider looking at clinical trials and reconsider taking a second type of chemotherapy drug—they saw the latest MRI and said it would not be good to wait and see what the next MRI shows—as a result, here is what has happened

Tom reached out to one of our neighbor's daughter who is at Duke—she was the Valedictorian of Keely's high school class and is a MD/PhD grad student at Duke and whose mentor is the neuro-oncologist who was the lead in Senator Ted Kennedy's brain cancer.

Our friend's daughter let her mentor know what has happened to date with Lucy.

The doctor offered his help and gave us his pager number—we talked with him and he suggested an immediate biopsy be done on the "enhancement"—he also suggested holding off on the second chemotherapy drug until we know the results since starting the drug may preclude us from trials—he said there may be trials he is working on that we may qualify for—he offered for us to come to Duke for the biopsy as well.

We have also reached out to another renowned brain cancer center and they are interested in looking at Lucy's case and have some trials—again great connections from Becky and Char.

We asked our oncologist, to reach out to the lead brain cancer doctor at CU Health Sciences for an appointment and discussion of trials she is aware of.

Last week we met with our neurosurgeon and the biopsy surgery was scheduled for Jan 31st.

The surgery was done Monday—Keely took off work and was with me at the hospital and a great support

Lucy came home this morning—she is doing fine and as ornery as ever

We won't know the results of the biopsy for a few more days as it was sent to CU for a read by their leading pathologist and the person who has done previous reads of Lucy's cancer

There was some good news from the biopsy surgery—there had been no enhancement from the MRI done 3 weeks ago and the MRI done right before Monday's surgery; this may be an indication that the chemo is being effective—however, the neurosurgeon did say that the 2 pieces removed for the biopsy definitely had cells that had characteristics of progression of the tumor. The neurosurgeon also patched a leak in the Dura near the incision from the previous surgery that was causing Lucy some swelling and headaches so this should help.

We are meeting with our oncologist tomorrow and once we know the results of the biopsy, our plan is to reach out to Duke, CU Health Sciences, and perhaps others and see what everyone thinks before deciding on a clinical trial or protocol as they are called. Lucy's next chemo regime starts Sunday and we'll see if the oncologist says to continue on.

Just wanted to let you know that we have shifted from wait and see to a very aggressive and proactive approach thanks to the doctors' suggestions to do so.

As always, we greatly appreciate all of the expressions of love and support—Lucy is resting and recovering from the surgery at home—she continues to be a real trooper as you would expect.

Love, Tom

February 3, 2011 Update
Good News

Hi everyone—some good news about Lucy—the biopsy came back today from CU Health Sciences and it is radiation necrosis—while there was a small amount of cancer detected, over 70% of the specimens were radiation damage or necrosis. Our oncologist said that this is good news because it means that the cancer is not progressing as fast as everyone thought and that the chemo may be holding the cancer at bay.

While very relieved, we know we are not out of the woods by any means; however what good news and it's my birthday and I have never had as good a present as the news about Lucy! For those guessing, I am not quite 6 decades. Enough about me . . .

I talked with the doctor from Duke today and he and our local oncologist will be talking over the next day or so to explore options and next steps. We are hoping for a trial here in Colorado but will consider all options.

Thanks for all of your love and support and the flowers today (gosh, I was vain enough to think for a nano second that they were for my birthday)—seriously, thanks to all and we'll keep you posted on next steps.

Our very best to you, love, Lucy, Tom, Keely and Kyle

March 5, 2011 Update

Hi everyone—even though March came in like a lamb (no sheep jokes just because we are Montanans); for Lucy it has come in like a lion. In our last update, we talked about starting to look at clinical trials. We reached out to Duke and CU Health Sciences. Our first consult was with the head of neuro-oncology at the Anschutz Cancer Center at CU Health Sciences, and their tumor board—we got the results this week. The good news is that the chemo and previous treatments are being effective at keeping the tumor that was removed and came back at bay. Also, they said Lucy is not a candidate for a trial at this point because the current treatments are being effective—with that info, we decided not to go to Duke since being at home is much preferred. They also said there are still options ahead of us with other chemo drugs, etc.

The not so good news is that there is a new enhancement on the other side of Lucy's brain that will be surgically removed next Wednesday. Yep, this is Lucy's 4th brain surgery and her 3rd in the past 7 months—she has the spirit of a lion as you all know but this makes us all nervous. The new enhancement is in the "silent" part of the brain and far from language and motor skills areas, so the Dr.'s are saying that there should be no real side effects from the surgery other than the normal recovery stuff which Lucy has mastered—she is getting a reputation at the hospital as the poster child for speedy and healthy brain surgery recovery; although she still complains to them that they still haven't sent her a fruit basket for all the business! It actually should be sent to my company for having such a great insurance plan!

If the enhancement is cancer, then Lucy will start another 7 week radiation and chemo regimen.

On the home front, Lucy and I went to LA to see Kyle and his performance in a play called "Wounded"—a take-off on the massacre at Wounded Knee. Kyle had the lead and we couldn't be prouder—not sure where he got the talent, but wow! We met the Director and the Playwright—both of them could not have been any more complimentary of Kyle. Seeing the play was one of Lucy's biggest wishes and we were so happy to do this.

Keely continues to add so much support here in Denver—she loves her landscape job and very happy to get teased by Spring being around the corner. She and Jake are moving to an apartment closer to our house so that is good. Both she and Kyle continue to grow as they deal with their mom's fight with cancer—it's just tough and we have definitely grown closer as a family.

I continue to work and have made arrangements with friends and family to be with Lucy when I have to travel. It's a tough balance, but fortunately, my travel is very manageable.

Lucy has lost much of her vision in her left eye from the previous surgeries and we are going to see a low vision specialist at CU Health Sciences to see if some special glasses with prisms will help—she has not been driving since December and this is yet another adjustment for such an independent person—navigating the airports last weekend was a very new experience for us both.

We'll let you know how the surgery goes and what the biopsy shows which may be 3-5 days after the surgery.

As always, we sincerely appreciate all of the expressions of love and support—your thoughts, prayers, spiritual good vibes, flowers, food, and just being here have meant so much to us—you are all part of Lucy's recovery and you are loved.

More to follow and do take good care everyone.

Love Tom, Lucy, Keely and Kyle

March 9, 2011 Update
Today's Surgery

Hi everyone—just a quick note to let you know that Lucy made it through her surgery in great shape—while we won't know the results of the biopsy for several more days, the surgeon told Keely and I that the tumor he removed looks a lot like the first tumor which is not great news—so I think we will be back for radiation and more chemo just like we did with the first tumor.

Once we know the results, we will let you know.

Keely and I both thought that Lucy looked better after today's surgery than she has looked on either of the previous 3—she also seemed much more coherent after today's—of course she was cracking wise with all the folks at the hospital and was in very good spirits in ICU when we saw her.

Many and continued thanks to all of you for your love and support—a neighbor and dear friend, Nancy surprised us at the hospital with my favorite peanut butter chocolate chip cookies. Thx Nancy!

After a very long day—I'll sign off early—take good care everyone!

Much love, Lucy, Tom Keely and Kyle

March 11, 2011 Update
Lucy Is Home!

Hi—just a very quick note to let you all know that Lucy is home and doing great as usual—she'll be getting some well-deserved rest—we have an appointment with the oncologist next Thursday and will have the official results of the biopsy—when we met with the surgeon yesterday, he told us that the preliminary results indicate that the tumor removed was very similar to the class 4 removed on the other side of her brain—given that, he told us to expect the same treatment plan which is 7 weeks of radiation with chemo once she fully recovers from the surgery.

The surgeon also said that Lucy beat the averages with her first tumor and there is every good indication that she will with this one.

Thank you all for your continued kind expressions of support—we'll be sure to keep you posted as we learn more.

My guess is that Lucy will be back to the keyboard sooner than later!

Much love and appreciation of your help—Lucy, Tom, Keely and Kyle

April 8, 2011 Update
More Fish to Fry

Hi everyone—I know many have been wondering what is going on with Lucy and thought to provide a quick update—since the 2nd tumor (left frontal) was removed on March 9th, Lucy has been having headaches off and on, as such, the oncology radiologist started her on steroids Tuesday of this week and the headaches have pretty much gone away—they also wanted a MRI done and that was done yesterday—unfortunately, the MRI showed that there is "normal tumor growth" in both areas where the tumors were removed—this is consistent with how the Glio's act—we are encouraged that the previous treatments have helped keep the first tumor at bay and that the same treatment will hopefully have the same effect on the 2nd tumor.

Lucy will start Chemo on Monday April 11th and combine it with radiation for 7 weeks in the area of the 2nd tumor that was removed.

So, we have more fish to fry as Lucy likes to say. Her spirits are good and even better now that the headaches seem to be under control.

We appreciate all of your continued expressions of love and support—Keely and Kyle are hanging in there and both continue to live their lives as Lucy and I want them to keep on keeping on. I am also hanging in there and even doing a little work travel—when I travel, Lucy will have a "slumber party" so you may be getting a call to see if you can spend the night with Lucy—it's not that she depends on having someone here 7/24 because she doesn't, it's more like an extra comfort for both her and me knowing she is not alone.

Again, many thanks for love, support, good vibes and prayers.

Love, Tom Lucy Keely and Kyle

CHAPTER 28

AS IF WE NEED MORE STRESS

Back in December 2010, I had received a reprieve from my new boss after he had tried to force me to quit and threatened to fire me. But, in May, he once again reared his ugly head—I say ugly because he never once asked me how my wife was doing or offered condolences after her death when I went back to work for a short time before resigning.

On a Friday in May, my boss let me know that I had 30 days to improve my sales performance or face being fired. Then, as if we didn't have enough stress, two days later on Sunday morning Lucy picked up the phone to take a collect call from the Los Angeles County Sheriff. Kyle was in jail after having been arrested for DUI. He had run into a street pole, totaled his car, and was lucky he hadn't been hurt or hurt anyone else.

I wanted to include this incident in my story because the accident turned into a real blessing for Kyle and our family. Kyle's stress level with his mom dying and the pressures of his second year in grad school had caught up with him, and my self-medicating had not provided him with the best role model[ii].

The day after Kyle got out of jail, he was home. This was a blessing, because it meant that Kyle was able to be with Lucy for the last months of her life, something that meant a lot to Lucy. His being here also helped us grow even stronger as a family leading up to Lucy's passing.

With my boss breathing down my neck, Kyle at home, and Lucy's health declining, I decided to exercise my rights under the Family Medical Leave Act (FMLA). This meant that I would have 12 weeks off with my job guaranteed upon my return, enabling me to be with Lucy full-time through her last breath.

During this stressful period, we received notification from the Social Security Administration that, beginning July 1, 2011 Lucy would be enrolled in Medicare. This would provide the health care coverage needed at a much lower rate than what was available through COBRA, Since I was on FMLA Leave during this time, I continued my regular health coverage at the lower price—again, finding out how Medicare works in conjunction with my current health plan was very helpful—information is power!

June 16, 2011 Update

Hi everyone! Hope all is well—just wanted to let you know that I have changed my email address since Qwest will no longer offer MSN, I am going to gmail—appreciate you changing me in your address book.

Two weeks ago, I finished my 7 weeks of radiation for the tumor that was removed in March—I am just starting to get the radiation sleeps—this means, I sleep a bunch! I continue to be on a chemo regimen of 21 days on chemo and 7 days off—the dosage is such that I am not having serious side effects so far. I am hoping to be able to make a trip north to Montana in late July to see friends and family.

As far as next steps in my treatment, we see the oncologist on July 7th and will get my next MRI scan in early August to see if the tumors are growing or not—not sure how long they will keep me on the chemo. So to make a long story short, my treatment plan is up in the air and will be based on what the MRI shows if anything. We are waiting to August for the MRI to give the area radiated time to heal.

The kids are doing fine—Kyle is home from grad school until mid-July and Keely continues her work in landscaping and we see her several times a week. Tom is taking some time off to be with me and I am enjoying him not traveling and working full time.

Wish I had more to report, but that's it for now—special thanks to my neighborhood girlfriends for bringing plants and their tools over a couple of weeks ago to plant flowers and do a general cleanup—the flowers and gardens are flourishing thanks to their help—we had a great time and it was good to see you all.

My very best to you and once again, thank you for all of your support.

Chat sooner than later, Love Lucy

July 7, 2011 Update
The "H" Word

Hi everyone and again, thank you for all the expressions of love and support!

Lucy's 7 weeks radiation for the 2nd tumor was completed on June 2nd—during the past 2-3 weeks, she has been experiencing some symptoms (headaches and trouble walking) that resulted in the oncologist ordering a MRI last week. These symptoms have kept Lucy away from email and that is why some of you may not have had replies—we hope to catch up soon. The MRI showed that the cancer from the 2nd tumor which was removed 3 months ago is growing. The treating radiologist told us that the growth is occurring in an area that they were not able to safely cover during the 7 weeks radiation treatment. The good news is that Gamma Knife (very focused radiation) can be used to treat the new cancer growth. Lucy will have the Gamma Knife procedure the morning of July 12th. Her 21 day on and 7 days off chemo regimen has been stopped until we learn more about the results of the Gamma Knife.

The other good news is that the first tumor removed in January 2009 that was treated with radiation, surgery, chemo and Gamma Knife is stable.

Well we heard the dreaded "H" word from both our oncologist and radiologist last week. Both suggested we at least enroll in Hospice in case as our radiologist (he is fighting his own 7 year battle with a blood cancer) said, get enrolled in case things go south quickly. We are going to meet with the Hospice folks but not enroll until we see how the Gamma

Knife worked. Our oncologist told us that once you enroll and start in Hospice that most treatment programs like chemo and radiation are not covered so that's why we are holding off.

Even with the H word, we are encouraged that the Gamma Knife will do as it did with the first tumor.

Lucy is doing better than can be expected and continues to remain positive and still full of her great humor and attitude. We spent a night at her good friend Char's mountain home last weekend and Lucy enjoyed getting out somewhere lots better than going to a Dr. Appointment.

We are still planning on getting Lucy to her dear Montana later in the month to spend some lake time with Gael and Doug at their Lindberg Lake cabin and head down to Billings to see the other members of the "Tall, Tight and Tan" trio, Phoebe and Kathleen. Of course we also see my mom, Paul and Carla and other friends and family. Keely and Kyle may join us if we can work it all out—the plan is to fly Lucy to Missoula and then fly her from Billings back to Denver while the rest of us drive.

We remain very optimistic and at the same time understand the realities of what we are fighting.

We know that many of you ask "what you can do to help?" Not sure is the best answer now—at some point we may get the meal on wheels going again—so do whatever you feel, whether it's saying a prayer, sending good vibes, a card, Nancy's noodle bowls, DJ's fun bag, Scottie's wine and chocolate or another Nancy's chocolate cupcakes! This is not a solicitation, I just want you to know we know you all care and it's hard to figure out what if anything you can do to help.

Best to everyone and I will keep you updated as we know more.

Love, Tom, Lucy, Keely and Kyle

CHAPTER 29

With both the oncology radiologist and oncologist suggesting that we enroll in hospice, I wanted to make sure I was well prepared to have a conversation with Keely and Kyle about what this meant. Lucy had fully understood what it meant prior to this point, though frankly, by this time she had lost some of her cognitive skills and was well into her decline.

As the primary family caregiver, it was critical for me to have as much information as possible about what was happening and what may happen throughout the entire fight—deciding when to enroll in hospice was no exception. My mother, in addition to being an RN and a retired nursing home director, had been a hospice volunteer for ten years. She provided me with some practical suggestions and information, and this, combined with the information packages supplied by the hospice provider, filled in all of the blanks.

Having a good deal of information about hospice really helped when me it came time to discuss the decision with Keely and Kyle. I wanted them to be involved in the decision about when to enroll in hospice because, as the hospice material suggests, many people think that once hospice starts, it means that all hope is gone. However, knowing what hospice does and does not do, this is definitely not the case. Hospice is not an irreversible decision. While it is true that cancer-fighting treatments are stopped when hospice is started, this does not mean that treatment cannot be restarted if the patient improves. It is possible to go off of hospice and then return later if needed.

By the time I spoke with Keely and Kyle, I was convinced that we needed to start hospice right away. More and more of my time was being focused on helping Lucy move around, eat, use the bathroom, and keep up with her hygiene, and frankly, I needed some help. For example, it wasn't uncommon for Lucy to try and get out of bed or off of the couch by herself when no one was around to help her, and sometimes she would fall. Fortunately she never got hurt, but it was becoming more and more difficult to lift her into the wheelchair or use the walker to get her either back in bed or back on the couch. The kids experienced some of these situations, which gave them a greater appreciation for what I was going through in terms of caring for Lucy, and helped them understand my position on hospice.

While Lucy was not totally bed ridden or incontinent, she was now wearing diapers and needed help with all movement. One of our neighbors, whose husband has multiple sclerosis, had a cool walker and portable wheel chair that she loaned us. Though Lucy never wanted to use the walker and didn't, the portable wheel chair turned out to be the best to help get Lucy around. Keely even took one of the old Montana license plates from the garage wall and attached it to the back of the wheel chair—Lucy really got a good laugh at seeing the license plate on her new mode of transportation.

In addition to installing grab bars in the bathroom, I also purchased an adjustable, portable bedside toilet. This device could be placed over the bathroom toilet, which made it much easier for Lucy since she did not have to sit as far down.

Even though I wanted Keely and Kyle's support in the decision on when to start hospice, I was fully prepared to make the decision by myself if they were not able to agree on a course of action or if there was too much push back. Again, while consensus was important, Lucy's comfort in her last days was my primary consideration.

After talking about it, we all agreed to use in-home hospice and decided to chat further about when to start after we got back from our Montana Seeley Swan Valley trip. In the meantime, I pointed Keely and Kyle to all the sources of information that I had received along the way. Reading the hospice material themselves helped both of my kids better understand what to expect.

CHAPTER 30

LUCY'S LAST HURRAH IN MONTANA

A s mentioned previously, one of the things that Lucy wanted to do before she died was take Keely and Kyle to the Montana lake country that she had fallen in love with as a teenager. They had both seen it several times before, but not as adults. In the summer of 2010, Lucy and I had spent a week at the lake cabin of some dear friends from Missoula, Gael and Doug. They were kind enough to invite us again, and Lucy had spent the last year wanting to take them up on their offer.

Before we left, I talked with the oncologist and his internist about the trip, and they both felt that whatever Lucy wanted to do and was able to do, was what she should do. Of course, by this time they had let me know that Lucy was experiencing end-of-life symptoms.

With Lucy on the decline, I decided that flying would be harder on Lucy than driving—besides we wanted to go on Lucy's schedule rather than the airline's schedule. In order to make the trip a little easier, I put together my special first aid bag, which included cleaning materials, the portable bedside toilet, and anything I would need to use to clean up after any accidents that Lucy may have along the way. This way I did not have to rely on my mom or Gael and Doug at the cabin for any cleaning supplies.

Early in our marriage, when I first started traveling a lot with my job, we decided to get a dog to provide company and a certain sense of protection for Lucy. Our close friends had two Airedale terriers, and we fell in love with them, so when one of their dogs had puppies, we took a look and went home with a female puppy that Lucy named Sage.

Sage was with us for over 12 years. Shortly after moving to Denver, Sage was diagnosed with cancer and given a short time to live. Lucy decided that for our summer vacation that year, we would give Sage one last hurrah and do the thing that Sage liked to do most—swimming in a lake. So, we made a plan to spend our vacation at Flathead Lake in northwestern Montana. Then, on the return through Billings, we would have Sage put to sleep by our favorite veterinarian, a man who Lucy called "Doc Hawk." Putting Sage to sleep after spending her last days swimming and before the cancer got horrific gave us great comfort. When Lucy said she wanted to go to the lake just one more time, I couldn't help but think of what Lucy had done for Sage.

We drove to Billings for the first leg of the trip and stayed with my mom. Lucy was pretty much confined to a wheel chair and slept most of the time. As a family, we had driven across Wyoming to Billings many times and certainly knew what to expect. With Lucy confined to a wheelchair, our main concern was her comfort and that included getting her to use rest stops along the way. This became really frustrating for all of us because Lucy refused to use any of the restrooms despite the fact that Wyoming has the nicest and cleanest rest stops of any state we had ever visited.

Keely, Kyle, and I tried every type of coaxing and persuasion available to us, but it was all to no avail. We all learned a new level of patience, but the situation was very hard on Keely and Kyle especially. The roles had been reversed, and instead of being parented by Lucy, they were the ones doing the parenting. As I write this, it brings tears to my eyes, because this was the one thing that Lucy had never wanted to have happen. Finally, we arrived at my mom's house. Before we had left Colorado, Lucy had put in a special request for my mom's fried chicken. Over the years, this had become her favorite dish that my mom made, and as a result, that was the first thing that we smelled as we entered the house.

Once we were inside, my mom took over as the primary care nurse—all of those RN graveyard shifts at the hospital, nursing home duties, and hospice volunteering just automatically kicked in. My mom was 86 years old at the time, but in good health and up to helping out.

In addition to my mom taking over as the primary nurse, she took the time to have some very candid chats with Keely and Kyle. She told Keely and Kyle, and then me separately, that Lucy did not have much longer to live. My mom has a way of being compassionately candid in matters that shouldn't, in her opinion, be sugarcoated. This was one of those matters. My mom's nursing, hospice, and nursing home experience had given her the ability to recognize that Lucy had reached her final decline.

Keely and Kyle were moved by the closeness with their grandma, and before we left for the lake, they asked if we could cut our stay at the lake by a day so that they could spend some more time with my mom.

Before we left for the lake, I called to check in with our oncologist's internist and told her what my mom had said. The doctor let me know that nurses, especially those with hospice or end-of-life experience, really can tell when the end is imminent.

Lucy was in good spirits, but the drive to the cabin at Lindberg Lake was quiet. I felt that, as each mile brought us closer to Lindberg Lake, the reality of this being Lucy's last hurrah set in not only for me, but also for Keely and Kyle.

Gael and Doug were there to greet us as we pulled into "Skunk Hollow," their beautiful lake space. Gael and Lucy were Kappa Alpha Theta sorority sisters, and Doug and I had been at the Sigma Chi fraternity house at the same time. While the four of us had fallen out of touch after college, we had rekindled the friendship five years earlier when Lucy and I had travelled to Missoula for homecoming. For some reason, the four of us had hit it off during that visit, and it was as if we had never lost touch.

Gael and Doug had raised their five children (four girls and a son) in Spokane and Bozeman before finally settling in Missoula, Doug's hometown. The Lindberg Lake cabin had previously belonged to Doug's father, a car dealer who had taken the property as payment for a car. Over the years, Gael and Doug had added a boat house with bunk beds onto the one bedroom cabin.

Keely and Kyle slept in the boat house, and Lucy and I shared the bed on the screened-in front porch. It was a gorgeous view of the lake and mountains beyond. Gentle breezes, water lapping at the shore, and a gazillion stars greeted us at night, and we woke to the sun peeking over the Swan Range beyond the lake. While we were there, Lucy spent most of the day in the bed or sitting in the porch, just taking in the beauty, or as her friend Phoebe would say, the "eye ball candy!"

The first thing that Gael asked Keely and Kyle was if they knew how to swim. Of course, she already knew that Keely had been a state qualifier in swimming, no small fete in a state with five million people. She also knew that Kyle had been a high school swim team member and did life guarding. Still, when they answered yes, she asked if they were really good swimmers. They again replied that yes, they were and then asked her why she wanted to know.

Gael explained that with all of the snowfall and cold weather, the lake was at its coldest for this time of the year since the 1970s. She then told us that the survival time in water that cold was nine minutes. Well, she may have embellished just a tad, but the next day, Keely was wearing a wetsuit on their paddle board as Kyle spent his time in the kayak.

With a little coaxing from Lucy, Keely and Kyle agreed to go tubing behind the boat. They shared the tube as Gael and Doug took them around the lake. Several times, they were bounced off of the tube and into the water. I'm guessing that Lucy knew that a little dump in the lake would suck the anxiety right out of them, even if only for a short time.

Doug really bonded with Keely and Kyle during our visit. He took it upon himself to keep them busy and took them on the hike that he had taken me on the previous summer—a nice, five mile round tripper to Holland Falls looking down on Holland Lake. Incidentally Lucy and I had enjoyed our first formal date at the Holland Lake Lodge in the spring of 1974 when I was her date to the Theta's annual "Daisy Picking" party.

Doug had been in the military before going to law school, and Keely and Kyle said that Doug was like a drill master and kept them moving quickly with short water breaks—Gale and her kids call him Captain Doug because of this trait. Even with his military background, Doug was especially great with Kyle, who is gay, and they had good chats about music and art. Doug had been in choir back in high school and, as a result, really knows his music stuff, and the two of them got along wonderfully in a very real and honest way.

While Lucy was napping, Gael took Keely and Kyle on a boat tour of Lindberg Lake and showed them the rock where Charles Lindberg had carved his name. Legend has it that, after flying over the lake on his way to a county fair in Missoula, he drove to the lake the next day and carved his name on a rock; "Charles Lindberg 1927."

Gale also showed the kids where the Swan River got its start—the mountain runoff from the Mission Mountains forms the Swan River which feeds Lindberg on one end and exits on the other end, making its way to Swan Lake, Lucy's childhood lake space, and then on to Flathead Lake.

Our time at Lindberg Lake gave Keely, Kyle, and I enough rest to face the difficult path ahead. It was clear to both Lucy and myself that her wish for Keely and Kyle to see and better understand the Montana that Lucy loved, had been realized.

The View from Lucy's Bed at Lindberg Lake

Back in Billings, we spent more time with my mom, my brother Paul, his wife, Carla, and the kids' cousin Joe. On Sunday night, we had dinner with dear friends. This gave Lucy the opportunity to see her Tall, Tight, and Tan Sisters, Phoebe and Kathleen, once more.

Seeing the Tall, Tight, and Tan Sisters together for what we all knew was the last time, was both joyful and sad.

Lucy smiled the entire trip other than when we tried to get her to use the rest stop bathrooms. Her smiles made it all worthwhile.

We got back home the evening of August 1st. Within two weeks, Lucy would be gone.

August 9, 2011 Update
Back from Montana

Hi everyone—in our last update we mentioned the "H" word and on Friday August 5th we enrolled in Hospice—for the time being we are doing Hospice at home so Lucy can be in her own bed and feel the comfort of her home.

During the week of July 25th we were able to take Lucy to her beloved Montana for some lake time and time with friends and family. This is something that Lucy really wanted to do and we ended up driving and having a great family road trip—Keely and Kyle had a great time with their mom and got to see what Lucy originally fell in love with in Montana—they also got to spend time with my mom and that was real helpful to us all. Lucy had a big smile on her face the entire trip! Lucy said that we need to start saving now for the 4 of us to fly instead of drive next year and of course as many of you know Montana has 2 seasons, Winter and Road Construction!

Special thanks to Gael and Doug for sharing their lake space and wonderful spirit of love and caring with us. They took Keely and Kyle boating and on a hike to Holland Falls. Attached are a couple of pictures from Harris' Skunk Hollow on Lindberg Lake. Lucy and I slept in their screened in front porch overlooking the lake with the Bob Marshall Wilderness and Swan Mountain Range in the background—each night we could look up in bed and touch the big dipper!

In Billings we had a wonderful evening with Paul, Phoebe, Kathleen and her husband Craige. Paul's culinary skills were great as always—it was nice to be back on Clark Avenue where we spent so many good times with Phoebe,

Paul, Kathleen, Barry and Shellie. Keely and Kyle enjoyed being with us for dinner. My mom cooked Lucy's special request of fried chicken and we had a good chat with her, my bother Paul and his wife Carla. The kids enjoyed being with grandma so much that we cut our lake time short to spend one more day with her. Carla fixed a fun travel bag which included all the goodies we could handle!

Over this past weekend, Lucy's sister Shirley and nephew Kenny came to visit and it was great to see them—Cousins Cindi and Stephanie also stopped by. Lucy's brother Tim is coming later and Shellie and Barry are coming up next week. Lucy even felt good enough to have Helen work on her neck and back which were really tight after all the driving.

On Sunday, Bistro Boys catering delivered a weeks' worth of food—a very special thank you to Char for her generosity and Pauli, her nephew who owns Bistro Boys (great food and service if you need catering in the future).

Again, many thanks to those not mentioned in this note for the flowers, books, dinners, goodies, calls, cards and expressions of love and support.

This is new territory for us and we hope to keep you all posted on how Lucy is doing—pls feel free to call me at any time if you have any questions—we may be re-starting the meals on wheels next week and will let you know.

Love to all, Lucy, Tom, Keely and Kyle

CHAPTER 31

Four days after we returned home, Keely, Kyle, and I all reached an agreement and pulled the trigger on starting in-home hospice. The hospice nurse was very professional and compassionate, and she explained that the primary goal of hospice would be to make Lucy's life as comfortable as possible. It was interesting to learn that hospice has a different set of dosage and frequency guidelines for pain medications than would normally be prescribed.

Once hospice care started, we still handled the day-to-day care, but it was nice to have additional support, and the nurse gave us some hints, tips, and training that were very helpful. In addition, I no longer had to worry about which doctor to call or whether or not it was necessary to call 911. Instead, I just had to place a call to hospice, and they would handle it, including dispatching a nurse right away if necessary.

The hospice coordinator also scheduled a meeting with the assigned social worker for the week following our return. This was designed to give us the opportunity to ask questions and express our concerns about care. The social worker was an independent source of information about hospice and end-of-life matters.

Having this independent source took some of the pressure off of me because prior to signing up for hospice, when one of my kids would ask a question, it sometimes came across to the kids that I was expressing my bias rather than just provide the information as I knew it.

By this stage, Lucy was pretty much bedridden. As I read the material from hospice, especially the part about how the body prepares itself for the final days, I was comforted to know that Lucy was getting closer and closer to her final breath. I pointed out the booklet to Keely and Kyle and told them that it was information that might help them better understand what was happening as it was happening, but I'm not sure if either one of them ever made the decision to read it as I did not want to make a big deal out of it.

During those last days, we talked about the fact that Lucy may want or need some type of reassurance from each of us that we would be all right when she died. At first, this was very tough to talk about with the kids, but once the signs and symptoms of Lucy's impending death became more pronounced, both kids worked very hard to let her know that they would be all right and that it was okay for her to let go.

CHAPTER 32

GOODBYES

The trip to Montana had given Lucy a chance to say goodbye to her friends and family there. It was very sad for all of us, knowing that this was the last goodbye, but everyone had tried to be upbeat and positive, especially for Keely and Kyle who would soon be experiencing one of the most difficult times in their lives. Lucy had always been the spark and spunk of our dinner parties in Billings, and it had been hard to see her when she wasn't at the top of her game, especially since she knew it. Although, after all of her treatments over the past 32 months, I wasn't sure how much of Lucy was really there during our trip.

After we got back to Denver, I made phone calls to Lucy's sister, Shirley, and brother, Tim, and let them know that I felt we were reaching Lucy's end-of-life. Shirley immediately made arrangements to come over the upcoming weekend, while Tim planned come the following weekend. Shirley's oldest child, Kenny, had also had a very close relationship with Lucy and decided to come and visit at the same time as his mom.

By this point, our families and close friends knew that Lucy was approaching death. It was very hard for me to see the looks in her friends' and family's eyes as they came for last visits—there were lots of hug and tears. The reality that the next time I would see many of these friends and family would be at Lucy's memorial service left me quiet and sad.

CHAPTER 33

U p until now, I had avoided making arrangements for cremation and for a priest to perform last rites. Looking back, I think it was my way of not giving up. But, on the 6th day of in-home hospice, I knew that it was time.

I got up Friday morning and called hospice to ask for a priest and then drove to a cremation provider that I had selected. I went by myself, not wanting either Keely or Kyle to have to go through this. At the time, both were still holding out hope for a miracle, but I think deep down they knew.

With the cremation plans taken care of, I waited for hospice to let me know when a priest would be coming. Before long, I got a call from Father Bill, who said he would be there in an hour. Keely was still at work, and I did not want to bother her—looking back at it, I should have waited until later in the day when Keely could have been there. Keely was fine with me getting this done in the morning, but I still sensed some hurt that I didn't include her.

Father Bill was kind and compassionate and told us that the rites were now called rites for the sick. After chatting with Kyle and me, he walked into the bedroom where Lucy was sleeping. He noticed the Montana license plate on Lucy's wheel chair and, noticing the county number that began the plate, asked, "Who is from Billings?" I replied that we all were from Billings, and he told us he had grown up in Roundup, just 60 miles north of Billings. It may have just been a coincidence, but it was somehow comforting, all the same.

I tried to wake Lucy, but she was sleeping very soundly. Father Bill told us not to worry about it, and he conducted the ritual of rites for the sick. He told us that it wasn't uncommon for the patients to be in similar states and that God was here regardless.

On Saturday, Lucy's brother Tim flew in from Salt Lake City. Lucy was bedridden and Tim spent time with her just holding her hand and talking.

Sunday was uneventful as Lucy continued to sleep without eating or drinking much. Because I had read the hospice material about how the body prepares for death, I knew that time was short before Lucy let go.

The hospice nurse had been in to check on Lucy and do some hygiene work. She told us to call at any time and left to see her other patients.

Tim left for the airport late in the afternoon. Keely, Kyle, Jake, and I had dinner. We were all quiet, and even without discussing it, I think we all knew that Lucy was close to letting go. We took turns going in and sitting with her. We would hold her hand and give her hugs. Lucy's eyes were open, but she did not say anything, more signs that she was close to letting go.

Around 7:30 PM, Lucy's breathing pattern changed dramatically as the hospice material had indicated would happen. Her breathing was shallow and irregular, but would speed up and become fast paced at irregular intervals. I sensed she was in some pain and gave her pain meds liberally as suggested by the hospice nurse. Keely was holding one hand, while Kyle held the other, and I had my arm around her. Jake had given us space.

I had called the hospice nurse. She told me she would be on her way as soon as she finished up with a patient and said that it may be and hour or more because she was coming from north Denver.

We elevated Lucy, and that seemed to provide short term relief. During all of this, Lucy was wide awake and kept looking at each of us kind of like she was making her rounds, staring into each of our eyes one at a time.

Before long, Lucy became congested and had to really fight for air. I gave her more pain meds. Her congestion was another known sign that passing was close—some call it the death rattle.

We all understood that the end was near, and each of us, in our own way, told Lucy that it was okay to let go and that we would be all right even though we would miss her dearly.

Suddenly, Lucy just started staring at me. Without any prompting, Keely and Kyle stood up and left the room. I held Lucy close, hugged her, and let her know that she was the one and only love of my life and that I was so happy to have had her. I told her that she should be very proud of being a wonderful mom and that I would take good care of Keely and Kyle and myself. Her breathing slowed, and on several occasions she stopped breathing for short periods of times. I kissed her and held her tight. She looked at me one last time and took one last breath.

I held her, knowing that she had just taken her last breath. I waited a couple of minutes before I kissed her again, once on the forehead and then on the lips. I said goodbye and told her that I would always love her.

It was 8:37 PM, and Lucy was gone.

The room was so silent, a silence that I will remember the rest of my life. After several minutes I went into the next room and told Keely, Kyle, and Jake that Lucy was gone. Keely and Kyle went into the room separately for their last goodbyes. We all hugged each other for the first time as a family of three.

I called the hospice nurse to let her know that Lucy was gone, and she showed up ten minutes later and took over. She let us know exactly what would happen next—she would prepare Lucy's body, take off any remaining jewelry, and tidy up the room. Within 30 minutes, two men from the crematory had arrived. In their black suits, white shirts, and black ties, they looked just like the movies had led me to believe they would.

They put Lucy on a gurney, covered her face, and asked if we wanted a last look. We had had already done that, so they wheeled her out of the house. During this time, the nurse took care of disposing of all the medications according to statue.

I made phone calls and managed not to have a meltdown. We were all in a state of disbelief, yet we knew the reality of what we had just experienced.

We talked, and I said that I was going to get rid of the bed because I could never sleep in the bed that had Lucy died in. After a while, Keely went into the bedroom and sat on the bed where Lucy had died. Later, she came out and said, "Dad, I felt such good energy in there that you must not get rid of the bed, ever."

I slept in the bed that night and have done so ever since. I still feel the spirit of Lucy and say goodnight to her each night.

Several days later, Keely and Kyle told me that when they saw their mom staring at me minutes before her death, they both felt she was trying to signal me. They believed that she did not want them to see her take her last breath and that she was telling me to have them leave the room. But, having their mom's instincts, they had left on their own, knowing that Lucy wanted it this way. Even with her last breath, Lucy was so Lucy.

August 15, 2011
Lucy in the Sky with Diamonds[iii]

> *Good morning everyone—our dear Lucy passed away last night about 8:30 having fought the good fight against this nasty cancer. Keely, Kyle and I were with her along with Keely's boyfriend Jake as her spirit and soul began a new journey. Lucy always had a deep faith in a greater power and on Friday received the anointment for the sick from a local priest, who happened to be from Montana.*
>
> *We are planning on having a memorial service here and one later in Montana—we will let you all know as soon as arrangements have been completed.*
>
> *Deep and heartfelt thanks to each and everyone of you for your love and support—while it is the saddest day of our lives life, there is joy in that Lucy is no longer in pain and now safe in a better place.*
>
> *Much love, Tom, Keely and Kyle*

CHAPTER 34

THE NEXT DAY

Monday morning came sooner than I wanted or expected. I felt the best thing to do was keep busy, and the first thing I did was send out the email on the preceding page—this time signing for the new family of three.

Besides sending out the email, I began the process of cleaning up the bedroom things I had not been able to deal with the night before.

I threw the sheets, mattress cover, and protective pad away and then flipped the mattress over—by early afternoon I had cleaned out the bedroom and removed the unused personal hygiene items, which I later donated. These small steps helped me get through the day, but all the while, I was thinking about the type of memorial service to have for Lucy.

I went through the jewelry that she had been wearing when she died, and I noticed that the gold cancer ribbon with small diamonds was missing from one of her necklaces. The charm had been a gift from Shirley, and Lucy had cherished it.

Frantically, I looked through the sheets, covers, and clothing, but to no avail. I moved the bed and went foot by foot over the entire bedroom floor with my hands and still did not find the ribbon. I called the crematory, and they said that they couldn't find the ribbon either. Then, a month later, I was picking out some socks from my dresser and stepped on something on the floor. I looked down, and there was the cancer ribbon—it had mysteriously shown up. The very next day, Shirley called and asked if she could have the necklace with the cancer ribbon that she had given to Lucy. I felt that, even in death, Lucy had not wanted to burden me with having to tell Shirley that the ribbon had been lost.

I completed short obituaries for the newspapers in both Denver and Billings—true to Lucy's request; I did not say anything like, "After a long and courageous battle with cancer . . ." I did, however, mention that she had died of brain cancer. Everyone who reads obituaries always wants to know what caused the deceased to pass, and I did not want any mystery.

CHAPTER 35

I wanted to have two memorial services; one in Denver and one in Billings. I knew my mom and other Billings folks would not be able to come to Denver, but I felt that it was important for us to feel the expressions of love and sympathy from my mom, extended family, and Lucy's Billings friends.

Lucy had never talked about what kind of memorial service she wanted, or if she even wanted one. As mentioned before, Lucy trusted me to do what I thought was best. I did know that, if we were to have a memorial service, she would want it to be a celebration.

It was easy to pick a day for the Denver service; I simply asked myself what would Lucy have done, and she would have had a "Friday at Four." Here is the note to Lucy's network for the Denver service:

> *Good morning everyone—just wanted to let you know that we will have a memorial service for Lucy at the Knolls Clubhouse located at 3200 East Geddes Drive, Centennial, CO 80122 on Friday August 19th at 4PM. We will also hold a service in Billings, Montana later next week.*
>
> *Lucy always looked forward to Friday at 4 to celebrate a good week and get a start on the weekend. Refreshments will follow the service. Again thank you for all of the love and support during this journey.*
>
> *Love, Tom, Keely and Kyle*

Here is the note to Lucy's network for the Billings service:

> *Hi all—in addition to a memorial service this Friday in Denver, we are doing a memorial service in Billings, Montana where we lived and Lucy has many friends and some family—the service in Billings is scheduled for Tuesday August 23rd at 11:00am at Shiloh United Methodist Church located at 1810 Shiloh Road—this is the church that my mom goes to and her help is greatly appreciated.*
> *Thx again for all your love and support.*
> *Best regards, Tom*

Rather than use the standard memorial service program provided by the cremation folks, I decided to create my own program. Tasks like this kept me busy and grounded during this tough time. When I was done, both the program and service felt right to me because I knew that Lucy would have loved both.

"Some of Lucy's Favorites

What goes around comes around

No vices no virtues

Don't answer a question with a question

Better take one for the team

Did you get some short term pleasure out of that?

Don't make me get the flying monkeys

Did you see that car?

Celebrating Lucy

Prelude	"Court and Spark"	Joni Mitchell
Seating of the family		
Welcome and Prayer		Becky Parnell, Friend
	Acolyte, Saint John's Episcopal Cathedral	
Lucy Living Life to the Fullest		Becky Parnell
Fond Remembrances		Shirley Reynolds, Sister
		Shellie Hochstadt, Friend
		Kyle Stockburger, Son
	"Climb Every Mountain"	
		Tom Stockburger, Husband
Group Prayer	"The Lord's Prayer"	Sally Tejan, Friend
Sacred Sound Healing with the Tibetan Singing Bowls		Helen Bruner Friend
Music to Reception	"Anniversary Songs"	Lucy made for Tom
		August 22, 2010

"Be still and know that I am God"
From the Mount Princeton warming cabin

Memorial Service Program

The facility for the Denver service had a room capacity of 110 people, but by several estimates, over 135 people showed up. True to form, after the service led by Shellie, one of Lucy's oldest and closets friends, ten of her closest girlfriends jumped into the swimming pool fully clothed as a tribute to Lucy's spunk and spirit.

On Sunday afternoon, Keely, Kyle, Jake, and I drove to Billings. We took our dog, Uma, and decided to stay in a historic hotel in downtown Sheridan, Wyoming rather than drive all the way to Billings. We got up the next day and had a leisurely drive to Billings.

By now, we were all running out of gas emotionally and just wanted the Billings service to be over so that we could go home. We decided that we would leave right after the 11:00 AM service on Tuesday.

The Billings service was well attended by many of Lucy's close friends, including the remaining members of the Tall, Tight, and Tan Sisters, Phoebe and Kathleen, who spoke at the service. My cousins and living aunt attended, and this really gave Keely and Kyle a deeper appreciation for the family that they were a part of. I was moved to see that my boss of 30 years ago and several bank clients from over 25 years ago had attended, as had my closest boyhood friends.

I did not pressure Keely or Kyle to say anything in remembrance of their mom at either service. I simple said that they were welcome to say something if that is what they wanted to do. Keely is much like her mom in that she keeps personal thoughts to herself—Lucy hadn't said anything at the memorial services for her father, mother, or her aunt, Ruby. Kyle is more like me and welcomed the opportunity to say a few words.

Kyle had given a wonderful remembrance of his mom at the Denver service and wanted to share at the Billings service as well. When Kyle's turn came to offer his remembrance, he stood up at the font of the my mother's church and said, "I never thought I'd be coming out in a church, my grandma's church, a church in my hometown, and at my mom's memorial service." He went on to describe how Lucy, knowing he was gay, had taken him to New York City for his 13th birthday to see Broadway plays and feel comfortable that gays are accepted in many places. Kyle also talked about the trip he and Lucy had taken to France to celebrate his 18ᵗʰ birthday and graduation from high school, and how they had stayed for ten days in one of the gay districts of Paris.

After the traditional post-memorial service lunch at the church, we got into the car to leave. As we were backing out of our parking spot, Keely asked in all seriousness, "So, now what are we supposed to do?"

EPILOGUE

K eely's question after the Billings service resonates with me to this very day, almost two years after losing the love of my life to brain cancer.

Keely married the love of her life, Jake, and is working fulltime in the landscaping business, where she pursues her passion for being outdoors and close to the earth. Kyle graduated with his Master's and bought a one-way ticket to New York where he is chasing his dream of working on Broadway.

I continue to see a grief counselor after Lucy's death. I quit my job after Lucy died, took a nine month consulting gig, and am now working fulltime in the same information technology industry I have been in for the past 36 years.

Writing this book has been primarily therapeutic in my healing process. Long ago in the early part of our marriage, I had entertained thoughts that one day I would write a book—I had no idea that Lucy's battle with cancer would end up being the catalyst.

A fitting close is my last thank you to Lucy's friends and family network:

> *One more thank you to all of you for everything you have done for Lucy and out family. I am deeply touched as are Keely and Kyle by the love and support from you all ... special thanks to those that helped with the services including those who shared fond remembrances, brought food, beverages, flowers, cards, and good vibes!*
>
> *What a journey—Lucy was right (once again) when she said I would miss her when she's gone. After 37 years with her in my life it has been a tough go since she left us—having said that, I know that when I get feeling blue, Lucy's voice inside me says, "keep on keeping on . . . or more bluntly, get over it*

and get to work . . . and remember, Keely and Kyle need their dad to be strong for both of us . . ."

Our family will be alright—a component of our healing process is and has been your support—besides, Lucy would kick my butt if we as a family did not get on with life. Even though there is a big hole in our hearts, Keely is back to work and Kyle back to grad school—as for me, well, I have decided to take some time off to figure out what's next—no, I am not selling the house and moving back to Lucy's and my beloved Montana at least not in the near term. In pure Lucy style, Lucy told all of her single friends here in Denver that I have no money, so I may have to move! Seriously, as we begin a new chapter in our lives, I wanted to share a write-up that was published in our neighborhood newsletter—written by dear friend Sally, it captures what many of us feel about Lucy.

Ta Ta for now and Much Love, Tom, Keely and Kyle

Here is the obituary that is referenced in my thank you email above. This was written by Sally G, a neighbor and one of Lucy's close friends. Sally had asked me to edit it before she submitted it but frankly, I made no suggestions as it was on the mark and so Lucy.

Long-time Knolls resident Lucy Reynolds Stockburger passed away on Aug. 14, 2011. She is survived by her husband, Tom, daughter, Keely, and son, Kyle. Many Knolls residents will recall seeing Lucy walking or riding her bike on the trails in the neighborhood, striding alongside the Knolls pool during summer swim meets or volunteering at political, charity and school events. She and Tom frequently welcomed friends into their home on Madison Circle for special evenings that included equal parts great food, lively conversation and intense laughter. Lucy had a keen interest in politics and proudly served as precinct chairwoman of Hillary Clinton's 2008 presidential campaign. As a licensed certified massage therapist, Lucy literally brought comfort and pain relief to her loyal clients, including many Knolls neighbors and residents. The healing power of laughter and

Lucy's keen insight into life were dispensed free of charge at each appointment. A conversation with Lucy might cover topics as varied as a new book, movie, play or concert, how to grow garlic and basil, the U.S. Open Tennis tournament, a challenging four-wheel trail in Colorado, a great little hotel or bistro in Paris and a current bargain at Costco. Lucy was an enthusiastic traveler and enjoyed exploring the high country of Colorado, neighborhoods of New York City or foreign cities. She approached trips with curiosity and managed to find humor in something odd or offbeat. Above all, she loved spending time with beloved family, friends and pets. Whatever Lucy tackled, she tackled with gusto and determination, including her fierce battle with brain cancer.

ABOUT THE AUTHOR

Tom Stockburger was born and raised in Montana and graduated from the University of Montana with a Bachelor's degree in Cultural Anthropology. He continues to work in the information technology industry as he has over the past 36 years. A proud father of Keely and Kyle, he is an avid reader, gardener, hiker, and tennis player, he has made the Denver area his home for the past twenty-five years, and shares his home with his dog, Uma, and his cat, Lily.

ENDNOTES

ii   I have Kyle's permission to share this story.

iii   "Lucy in the Sky with Diamonds" is a song written by John Lennon and Paul McCartney that was recorded by The Beatles for their 1967 album Sgt. Pepper's Lonely Hearts Club Band.